From charm bracelets to greeting cards and necklaces to headbands, you'll find a whole host of practical ways to use your beaded masterpieces.

Foreword

Beadwork is an exciting and fulfilling hobby. I was lucky enough to discover it at a relatively young age, thanks significantly to my mom, who always kept us both busy with any number of creative projects. My favorites were always the ones that involved beads or any other tiny treasures.

Now I am forever thinking of ways to turn everyday items into little beaded works of art. There are always new techniques to explore, new beads to discover, and new inspiration to be found.

Whether it is a slice of watermelon, a random color combination from some bead soup, or a visit to one of my favorite places, I find inspiration in almost everything. I hope this book will help you to enjoy the limitless beading possibilities in the world around you.

Amanda Brooke Murr-Hinson

About this book

Section 1:
Tools, supplies, and techniques

The book begins with some basic information on the variety of beads, wire, findings, and other materials that are available. You will also find information on useful tools to have, plus guidance on key techniques and handy hints on overcoming problems, such as bent wires.

Section 2:
Pattern selector

The pattern selector gives a great overview of all the beaded miniatures that you can create. Cast your eye over each vibrant spread and select your chosen pattern to bead up. Once you have decided, all you need to do is turn to the page listed beside it for a full set of instructions.

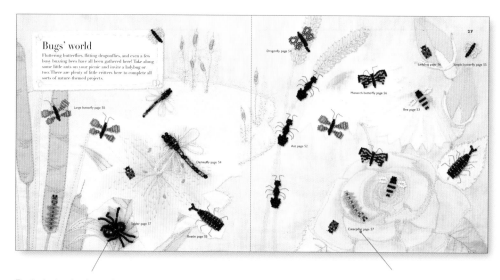

Each design is shown in proportion to the other pieces on the spread; this way you get a sense of size and scale.

Each pattern gives the page number where you can find its assembly instructions.

100 Beaded Flowers, Charms & Trinkets

100 Beaded Flowers, Charms & Trinkets

PERFECT LITTLE DESIGNS TO USE FOR GIFTS, JEWELRY, AND ACCESSORIES

Amanda Brooke Murr-Hinson

St. Martin's Griffin
New York

Library of Congress Cataloging-in-
Publication data available on request.

ISBN: 978-0-312-59141-0

First U.S. Edition: January 2012

Conceived, designed, and produced by
Quarto Publishing plc
The Old Brewery
6 Blundell Street
London N7 9BH

QUAR: BEMI

Senior editor: Lindsay Kaubi
Text editor: Liz Jones
Art editor and designer: Susi Martin
Photographer: Phil Wilkins
Illustrator: Chris Taylor
Fabric illustrations: Jessica Kinnersley
    www.jkinnersleydesigns.co.uk
Art director: Caroline Guest

Creative director: Moira Clinch
Publisher: Paul Carslake

Color separation by Modern Age
Repro House Ltd., Hong Kong
Printed by 1010 Printing International
Ltd., China

10 9 8 7 6 5 4 3 2 1

(handwritten: occ 11/6/12   745.58   BRO)

Contents

Section 3:
Beading patterns

This is where you will find the instructions and clear illustrations on how to put together your beaded miniature. As well as finding out how to assemble your pattern, you can see the finished article you want to achieve. In some cases, color variations have been included, to show you the endless beading possibilities.

This finished example appears at actual size.

Each pattern has been given a rating in terms of its difficulty (easy, intermediate, or challenging).

Alongside each pattern there is a list of the number and color of the beads used. Unless otherwise stated, all beads used are sized 11/0. The tools and supplies required are listed here also.

The clear illustrations show the path that the wire should take in order to complete the pattern.

Details of the different techniques that have been used in the pattern can be found here.

Section 4:
Projects

Once you have completed a pattern, the projects section can help you find a fun way of showing off your work. This section is designed to inspire you and show you finished articles that you can replicate, whether it's a headband, necklace, or greeting card.

These spreads showcase completed projects and give simple instructions on how to put them together.

Section 1:
Tools, supplies, and techniques

Beads

15/0   11/0   8/0   6/0

There is an almost endless variety of beads available. Every color you can imagine can be found, and they can be made from many different materials. Stone, clay, glass, crystal, bone, wood, and acrylic are only a few of the materials used to create beads today.

The type of beads used in a project will greatly influence its overall finished look. Faceted crystal beads can be used for beautiful, sparkling wedding projects, silver-lined glass beads are gorgeous for Christmas projects, and beads with a matte finish make for some beautiful modern motifs.

Bead shape

There is a huge array of choices when it comes to bead shapes. There are basic geometric shapes such as rounds, cubes, and bicones, along with discs, nuggets, and bugles, but there are also endless varieties of fun shapes such as hearts, stars, and animals. Some beads can even be very detailed and shaped like cupcakes, high-heeled shoes, birds, and even snowmen and pots of gold.

Seed beads

The smallest types of beads, Rocailles or seed beads, are available in round, hex cut, cubes, triangles, bugles, drops, peanuts, and even tiny little tiles.

Japanese round seed beads are often preferable to other beads since they have a more uniform shape, a large hole to accommodate wire passes, and a greater variety of available colors. Czech seed beads are less expensive, but the shape is not as consistent, and the holes are much smaller, which can be difficult when passing wire and string through them multiple times. There are also Japanese cylinder beads, but they create a more squared, boxy finished piece, which can take away from the delicate smoothness of miniature motifs. Cylinder beads can also be quite expensive.

Seed bead size

Seed beads come in a variety of sizes. The three most popular and widely available are 11/0, 8/0, and 6/0. Size 11/0 beads are the smallest of those three, with 6/0 being the largest. As you can see, the higher the number, the smaller the size of the actual bead. If you are just getting started with seed beads and making beaded miniatures, it's a good idea to use size 6/0 beads until you get the hang of working with the beads and wire. Since size 6/0 beads are the perfect size for ornaments and gift tags, you can present your practice pieces as gifts to friends and family. As you become more comfortable with the techniques, you can start working with size 11/0 beads, which can be a bit tricky, but will produce adorable miniature motifs. In this book, we will mostly be using size 11/0 round glass seed beads for the motifs, with a variety of other beads used in the finished project designs.

Bead size
Different bead sizes are required for different types of projects. For example, size 11/0 seed beads are great for earrings and charm bracelets. The larger size 6/0 seed beads make wonderful ornaments and gift tags.

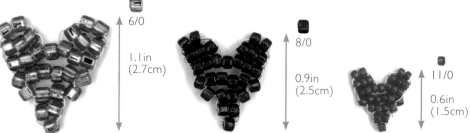

6/0   1.1in (2.7cm)

8/0   0.9in (2.5cm)

11/0   0.6in (1.5cm)

AB finish

Matte opaque

Transparent

Glass opaque

Translucent luster

Silver-lined

Bead types

The beads used for the beaded miniature designs in this book fall into three categories: rocailles, glass, and crystal.

Rocailles (also called seed beads)
Rocailles—small round seed beads—offer the greatest variety of colors and finishes and form the basis for all the beaded miniatures in this book.

Crystal
Crystal beads will add sparkle and elegance to your beaded motifs.

Bead finishes
Even if they are all the same color, beads with different finishes reflect the light in a variety of ways—so there is a noticeable difference in tone between them.

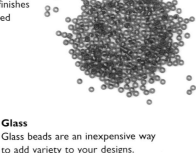
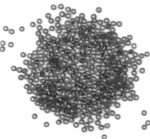

Glass
Glass beads are an inexpensive way to add variety to your designs.

DESIGN TIP
Transparent beads can sometimes fade into the background if used next to darker opaque beads. String a few beads of different finishes next to each other on some wire to see how they look together before using a large amount in your motifs.

Color

Color is probably the single most important element when designing miniature, beaded motifs. Getting the bead colors as close as possible to the real-life object the motifs are based on will make all the difference to your designs. It can be helpful to carry inspirational pictures with you, and use those to select colors for your projects when shopping for beads.

One important consideration is that even one single color can be available in many different shades and finishes. Take green, for example. There are opaque green seed beads in both a shiny and matte finish, as well as transparent and translucent green in both shiny and matte finish. And let's not forget the silver-lined green, alabaster opal green, green inside color, green aurora borealis (AB) finish, Ceylon green, and metallic green seed beads. For most basic designs, opaque beads are usually the best choice. Both the shiny and matte finishes can lend more realism by reflecting the color palette of the original items. However, when it comes to your own themed pieces, such as beaded fairytale castles or flip-flops, the sky is the limit! Bright silver-lined, shiny metallic, and glowing alabaster opal beads will bring a great deal of distinctive fun to your beaded miniatures.

The most important thing to remember is to choose colors that you like. You do not have to use the exact colors in the patterns in this book. By choosing your own colors, you can create cupcakes in your favorite flavors, daisies in your favorite colors, and birthday balloons to match your own party theme! There are many motifs in this book that can be customized to your own taste.

THE COLOR WHEEL
The best tool to help you with color is an artist's color wheel. It shows all of the primary (red, yellow, blue) and secondary (green, orange, violet) colors. The position of each color on the wheel determines how it reacts with others. Colors opposite each other are called complementary colors. They create striking contrasts when placed side by side.

Wire, findings, and other materials

Wire is the backbone to every design in this book, and findings are often the finishing touch, so it's important that you choose the right wire and findings for your project.

WIRE GAUGE

Wire is either sold in gauge (ga) or by millimeters (mm), both of which refer to its diameter. The gauge commonly used is American Wire Gauge (AWG). Although these don't match up exactly, a rough conversion is usually close enough for most wirework.

AWG	mm
38	0.1
36	0.13
34	0.15
32	0.2
30	0.25
28	0.3
26	0.4
24	0.5
22	0.6
21	0.7
20	0.8
19	0.9
18	1

Wire

For the motifs and projects in this book it is recommended that you use craft wire instead of sterling silver or gold-filled wire. Craft wire is less expensive and comes in many different colors. It is also often easier to work with, and less prone to breakage. However, you should feel free to use whatever kind of wire you desire.

Wire size and gauge

Wire size is measured by its diameter, and will be listed by gauge or mm. The size most commonly used for the motifs in this book is 30 gauge (0.25mm). This size works very well with the 11/0 seed beads.

Nylon beading thread

Pick a thread that will fit easily through your needle, in a color that matches the beads you are using. It is also possible to use a contrasting color if it fits in well with your design. Generally though, you want your beaded motif to stand out more than the thread on your appliquéd pieces.

Larger seed beads will require a thicker wire to help the beaded motif to hold its shape.

Wire color

For most of the beaded miniatures in this book, it is recommended that you use non-tarnish silver wire. It is a little more expensive than tinned copper (silver-plated copper) but it will keep its silvery shine much longer. Other colors may also be used to blend in with the beads, such as green wire for leaves, or orange wire for little goldfish. Or you could use a complementary color in your designs that enhances the look of the finished piece.

Choosing metals

Silver-plated wire is a lot cheaper than the real thing. It is popular due to its color, shine, ease of use, availability, and price. But look out for other color-plated metals to complement or contrast with your beads.

Findings and materials

After you have made up a batch of miniature beaded motifs, you will wonder what to do with them all! With only a few findings, some fabric or ribbon, and a little creativity, you will be making beautiful finished projects in no time.

Kilt pins

Kilt pins make wonderful accessories for backpacks and purses. You can attach several of your favorite beaded charms, and accent with matching dangles.

Split rings

These are coils of metal (like a key-ring), which are harder to open than jump rings but cannot be pulled apart, so are much more secure. Use them as one end of a clasp with a lobster or trigger clasp, or use them to attach a clasp to a bracelet.

Ear studs

Ear studs provide a simple base for small earrings. You should use a strong jeweler's glue to attach your finished beaded motifs.

Ear wires

Ear wires come in many different shapes. French ear wires, or kidney ear wires, are the most versatile, but you can choose the one that best suits your motif and personal style.

Jump rings

Jump rings are used to turn your beaded motifs into charms. You can easily add them after the motif is finished. Another option would be to add a soldered jump ring on the wire between the beads on the top row of the design when beading your motif.

Ring blanks

Make sure to use a ring blank that has a pad close to the size of the beaded motif. You don't want any of the base pad showing around the edges of the motif; however, you also do not want the base pad so small that the motif hangs over the edges and gets bent and distorted.

Earring hoops

Earring hoops make a wonderful base for wine glass charms. It is a good idea to check and see that the size hoop you are using will fit around your wine glass stems first. Larger hoops can be cut down to size if they seem too big.

Head pins

These can be used as support for beads when making earrings and pendants or for when you are adding beads to kilt pins. The flat head of the pin prevents beads from falling off.

Bar pins

These come in several different sizes. Make sure to choose the correct size for your finished motif. Also make sure that your bar pin has holes in it because this makes it much easier to weave the motif to the bar using wire.

Chain bracelet

There are many different styles and sizes of chain available. You can pick one that suits your own style and matches the charms you plan on adding to it. Small silver-plated chains are a good choice because they are so versatile.

Tools

Use good-quality tools. Inferior tools are often uncomfortable to use, can damage your wire and findings, and will not last as long as better-quality products.

You do not need very many tools to make the beaded motifs in this book. A good pair of wire cutters is the only essential item, and as thin as the wire is that you will be using, you could possibly get away with using a sturdy pair of scissors to trim your wire ends. But be advised that this will spoil your scissors, so don't go using your best pair of antique sewing scissors.

If you plan on making a lot of larger motifs using size 6/0 beads and a thicker wire, you may want to invest in a more heavy-duty pair of wire cutters. The thicker wires will dull the small nipper tools much quicker than if you are using a strong pair of end cutters. Button shank removers are a great inexpensive alternative to wire cutters.

Beading tools

Wire cutters/side cutters
A good pair of wire cutters is essential to any of the motifs in this book. Side cutters, sometimes called nipper tools, are recommended because you can cut very close to your work, and avoid having little stray wires poking out.

Nylon-jaw pliers
Use these to straighten out bent and crooked wires without scratching the wire. These are very good for smoothing out the end of your wire (shown below) to make it easier to slide through the rows of beads.

Round-nose pliers
Round-nose pliers are great for pulling stubborn wire through a row of beads. They can also be used to assemble many of the finished projects in this book.

Beading needles
There are a large variety of beading needles to choose from. Longer needles tend to allow for more control. Just be sure that whatever needles you use have a small eye to fit between the rows of beads in the finished motifs.

Memory wire shears
These special cutters are essential for cutting memory wire, which is very resilient. Regular wire cutters and cutters could be damaged if used with memory wire.

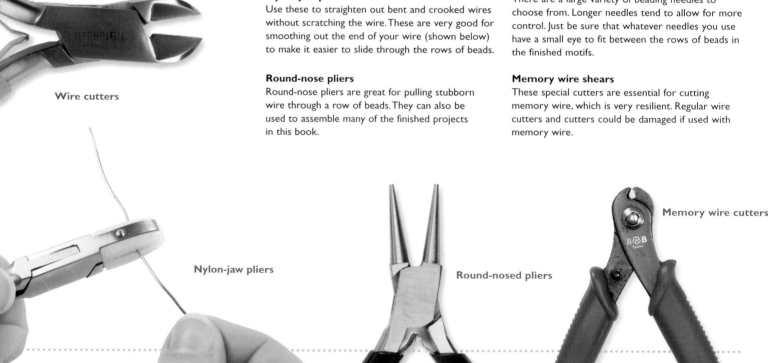

Wire cutters

Nylon-jaw pliers

Round-nosed pliers

Memory wire cutters

Other supplies

Sewing needle
Beaded motifs can be used to adorn your scrapbook pages. Use a sewing needle to make holes in your scrapbook pages so that you can wire your beaded motifs to the pages wherever you want them. Make sure the needle you use is sharp enough to pierce the paper, and will make a large enough hole for wire to pass through.

Bead mat
Bead mats make a great work surface. The fibers stand up just enough so that they do not allow your beads to roll around everywhere, but they do not stick up so much that your beads will get buried in the mat.

Bead mat

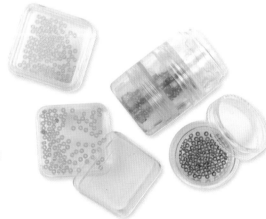

Storage

Tool storage
One way of storing tools is to put them in a spinning kitchen utensil storage unit. That way you can easily grab what you need without having to dig around in messy drawers or boxes. A paintbrush holder, available from art and crafts stores, is another good solution.

Bead storage
Seed beads can be stored in the clear plastic tubes in which they are often sold. A set of clear plastic drawers works well for storing the tubes because they can be laid down flat and, if they are organized by color, you can quickly pick out the exact shade you need.
Other beads, such as pressed glass and crystals, can be stored in little plastic grip seal bags.

Wire rounder
This is an optional, but helpful tool if you want to smooth or "round out" the ends of your wire.

Lighting
The best light to work by is natural sunlight. If you can't work near a window, or are working at night, it is essential that you have another source of good lighting, especially when working with tiny seed beads. Daylight bulbs and full-spectrum lights designed specifically for crafts can be purchased easily—some lamps even come with convenient detachable magnifying lenses—but any light bulb that produces full-spectrum lighting will work. Bad lighting can damage your eyes.

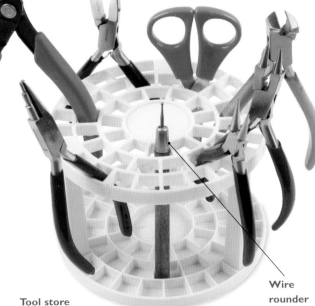

Tool store

Wire rounder

Core techniques

Each beaded miniature featured in this book is made using one basic technique, where wire is woven through consecutive rows of beads. How you arrange, or line up, your rows of beads and the path that your wire takes will determine what the finished piece looks like.

Threading beads on the wire

To add beads quickly to the wire you're working with, lay the beads out on a bead mat, and gently point the end of your wire through the holes of the beads you need. The beads will pop up onto your wire, and you can move beads further down on the wire.

BEAD TIP
You can paint one end of your wire with a brightly-colored nail polish to help you remember which side you are working with. For example, you could paint one side with red to coincide with the patterns in this book. Then you will always know which side of wire you are working with, and where that wire needs to go.

Basic construction

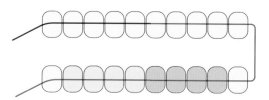

1. To begin, string all the beads needed for the first row of your pattern onto the wire. This example uses the Battenberg cake pattern (see page 64). String 10 cream beads for the top row.

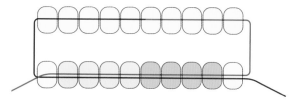

2. For the second row, string 1 cream, 4 pink, 4 yellow, and 1 cream onto the right (red) side of the wire protruding out of the 10 cream beads.

3. Take the left-hand side wire (blue) that is coming out of the 10 cream beads on the first row, and take it through all the beads in the second row, in the opposite direction to the wire that is already going through the beads.

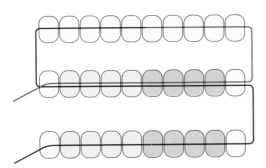

4. Add the beads for the third row to one side of the wire (either red or blue), making sure the bead order follows the pattern, and then insert the opposite wire through the third row in the opposite direction to the first wire.

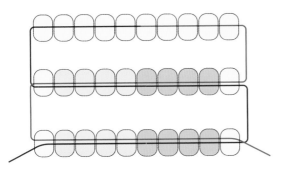

5. Continue in this fashion until the pattern is complete.

Reading the beading patterns

Unless otherwise noted, one single length of wire is used in each pattern. Opposite ends of the wire are color-coded to help you follow the path the wire is taking through the beads. The first row will be marked as the "start."

 Although the patterns in the book range from very simple to relatively complex, as soon as you have mastered the basic method of construction, it will be quite easy and lots of fun for you to complete any of the patterns, or even create your own. The next few pages explain the basic technique needed for each pattern and how to construct multiple-component motifs.

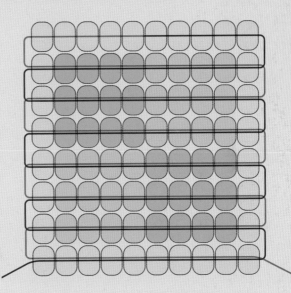

In this pattern you can see how the length of wire runs through the beads in the pattern. One single piece of wire is used, and each beginning side of wire is represented by a different color.

Finishing and securing a beaded motif

When you come to the end of making a beaded motif, remember not to trim your wire right away. You will need to wrap your wire ends into the beaded motif to secure everything in place. Take one end of the leftover wire, and carefully weave it between the wires on the sides of the beaded motif. After you have woven through three to four wires, use your wire cutters to trim the wire close to the beaded motif.

If you do not want the bulk of extra wire showing on the sides, you can begin weaving the wire back through the rows of beads until the miniature is secure. This works well when using the thinner wires or larger beads.

Joining beaded sections

Sometimes it is easier to bead different sections of a miniature separately and join them after they are each completed. This allows for "hinged" miniatures that can open and close.

To do this, simply bead each section as usual, finishing and securing the ends as always. Next, using a thinner gauge of wire (32 or 34 gauge, 0.2 or 0.15 mm, works well), weave the sections together at the join.

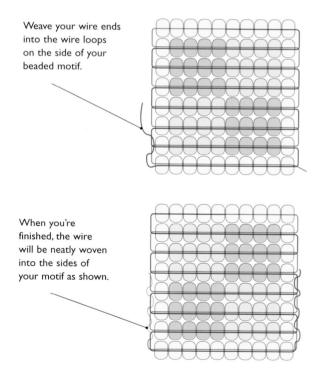

Weave your wire ends into the wire loops on the side of your beaded motif.

When you're finished, the wire will be neatly woven into the sides of your motif as shown.

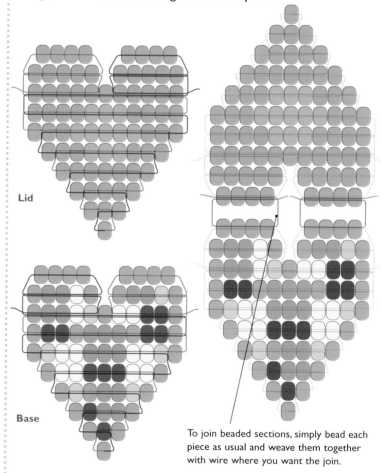

Lid

Base

To join beaded sections, simply bead each piece as usual and weave them together with wire where you want the join.

Adding wire appendages

After completing the base of the beaded motif, you will use the appropriate colored wire and go back through several rows of beads. To do this, take a small length of wire (about 5–6in, 13–15cm) and run it through the row below where you want your wire appendages to come out. Center the beaded motif on the length of wire so that you have an equal length of wire coming from each side of the row of beads. Take the right length of wire, and pass it through the row of beads above the initial row. Do the same for the left length of wire. Now you should have wire coming out of both ends of the correct row. Last, trim the ends to the desired length. Repeat this for each appendage.

Trimmed wire appendage

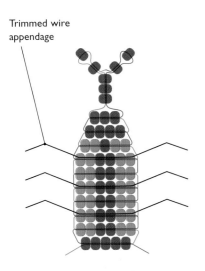

How to straighten a wire

If your wire has bent into a loop, you will be able to work the kink out if you coax it gently.

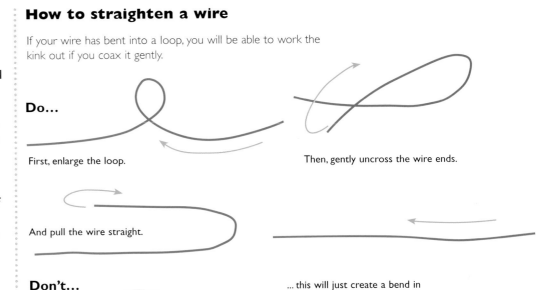

Do...

First, enlarge the loop.

Then, gently uncross the wire ends.

And pull the wire straight.

Don't...

Don't try to pull the loop tighter...

... this will just create a bend in the wire and it may break.

How to add a jump ring

Adding a jump ring is very simple and creates many possibilities for your finished beaded motifs. Simply open the jump ring, loop one open end between two rows of beads in your motif, and close up the jump ring using round-nose pliers. In most cases, it is best to add the jump ring between the top and second row of the finished beaded motif. This way it will hang properly.

Flower assembly

Clematis

This technique is used for the Clematis (page 69), Dog rose, Tulip (both page 70), Poppy (page 73), and Pansy (page 74). The other flowers are assembled according to their own individual patterns, and instructions are included on the pattern pages.

Dog rose

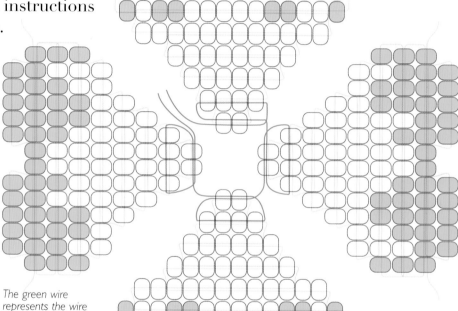

The green wire represents the wire used to weave the petals together.

2. Take a separate length of a 32 or 34 gauge (0.2 or 0.15 mm) wire and weave it through the bottom two rows of each petal, until all petals are connected. Secure ends as usual.

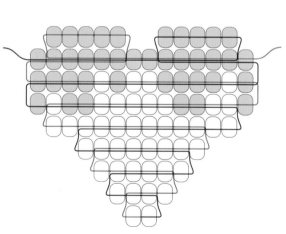

1. First, assemble each flower petal and components as usual.

Tulip

Pansy

Poppy

Adding flower centers

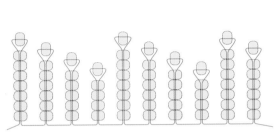

3. Make the center of the flower, as the pattern requires.

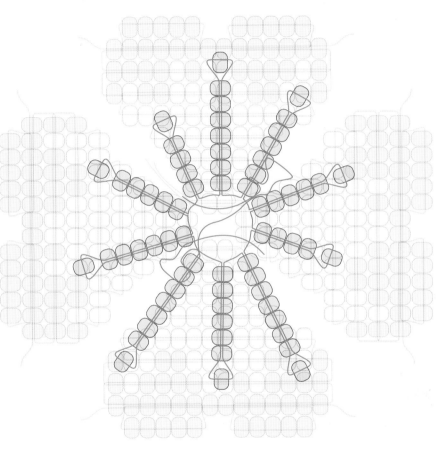

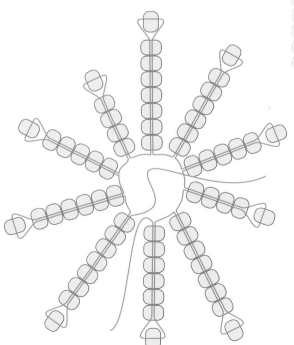

4. When the center is complete, do not trim the extra wire. Instead, use the two lengths of extra wire from the center to weave it into the inside edges of the petals. Then secure and trim the wire as usual.

Section 2:
Pattern selector

Bugs' world

Fluttering butterflies, flitting dragonflies, and even a few busy buzzing bees have all been gathered here! Take along some little ants on your picnic and invite a ladybug or two. There are plenty of little critters here to complete all sorts of nature-themed projects.

Large butterfly page 55

Damselfly page 54

Spider page 57

Beetle page 53

Dragonfly page 54

Ladybug page 56

Simple butterfly page 55

Monarch butterfly page 56

Bee page 53

Ant page 52

Caterpillar page 57

At the beach

What could be more relaxing than to spend a day by the sea? Walking through the sand in your flip-flops, and relaxing under an umbrella while watching sailboats glide by. You may even catch a fish or two! Remember to keep a beady eye out for those sneaky little crabs!

Umbrella page 63

Starfish page 59

Flip-flops page 63

Seashell page 59

Lighthouse page 60

Palm tree page 60

Sailboat page 62

Crab page 58

Shovel and pail page 62

Fish page 61

At the diner

When you get hungry, there's a delicious spread waiting! From sweet to savory, it's all here: scrumptious entrées followed by delicious desserts. Just imagine little beaded popsicle earrings, charm bracelets adorned with miniature sushi slices, or a cute little pizza slice necklace. Grab your needle and wire and start beading!

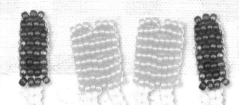

Popsicles page 68

Bubble tea page 65

Sushi roll slices page 67

Pizza slice page 67

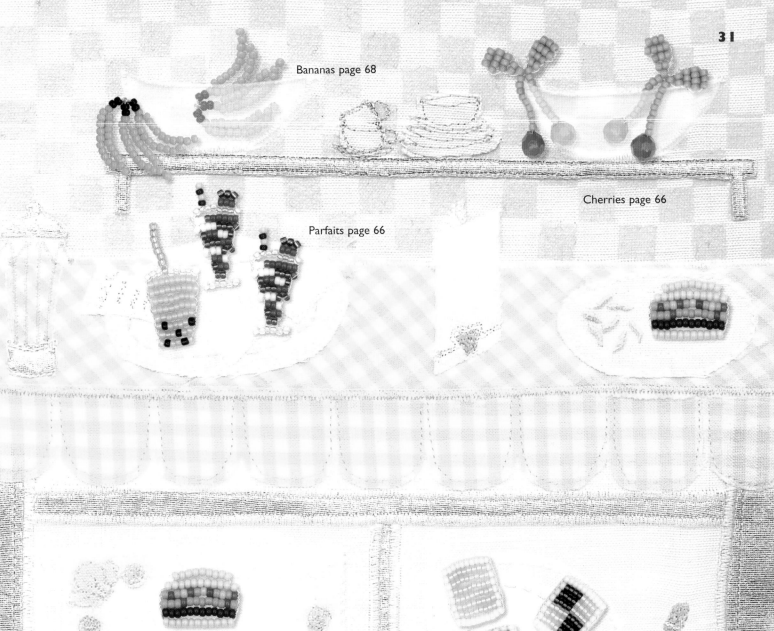

Bananas page 68

Cherries page 66

Parfaits page 66

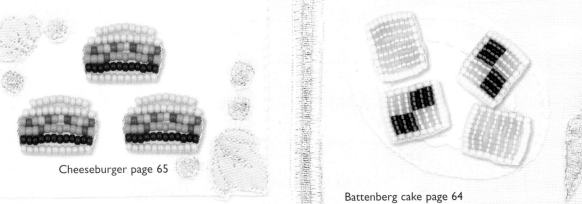

Cheeseburger page 65

Battenberg cake page 64

In the garden

Come take a walk through this lovely beaded garden, where there are so many shimmering flowers in gorgeous colors. These beautiful blooms will look great during any season, and are sure to last a lifetime. Mix and match them to create your own beaded bouquets.

Clematis page 69

Tulip page 70

Pansy page 74

Morning glory page 73

Fuchsia page 72

Dog rose page 70

Poppy page 73

Daisy page 71

The bakery

A stop in this pastry shop is sure to delight; delectable sugar cookies, delicate macaroons, and delicious dipped strawberries are all to be found here. And let's not forget the cupcakes. These make perfect little charms for party favors or birthday greeting cards.

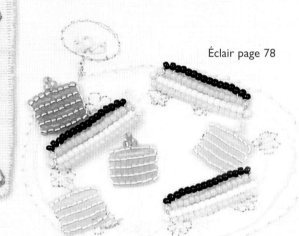

Éclair page 78

Petit fours page 77

Heart cookies page 76

Macaroons page 76

Cupcakes page 78

Dipped strawberries page 75

Party ring cookies page 79

Ice-cream cones page 77

Mouse page 86

Nature trail

Time for a little wander through the woods; perhaps we will catch a glimpse of a fox, a deer, or maybe even a gnome! Take inspiration from a woodland walk to bead tiny toadstools and cute little acorns. Add findings to create playful earrings, bracelets, or rings.

Fox page 83

Apple tree page 8

Toadstool page 83

Gnome page 81

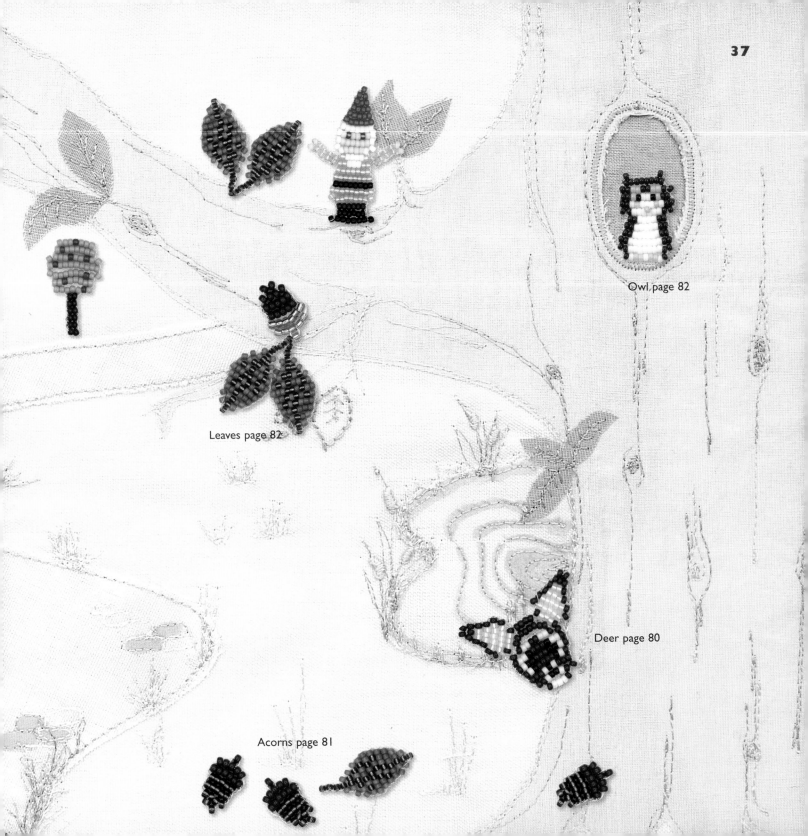

Owl page 82

Leaves page 82

Deer page 80

Acorns page 81

37

Animal crackers

It's a mini menagerie; bead up lots of these tiny little animals to create your own miniature zoo! From tiny turtles to mischievous monkeys, you are sure to find the perfect creature for your project.

Fox page 83

Mouse page 86

Rabbit page 88

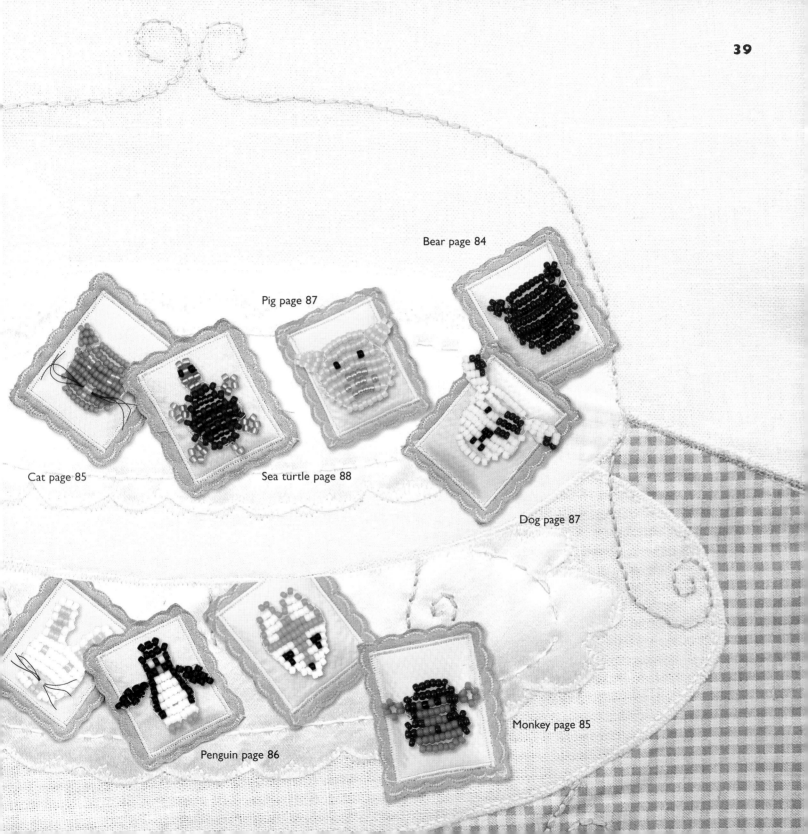

Bear page 84

Pig page 87

Cat page 85

Sea turtle page 88

Dog page 87

Penguin page 86

Monkey page 85

Happy holidays

The Christmas lights have been strung and the tree is ready for Santa. Don't forget to hang up your stockings! These holiday-themed trinkets make wonderful adornments for Christmas cards and scrapbook pages, or even as decorative gift tags.

Santa page 93

Snowman page 89

Christmas ornaments page 91

String of Christmas lights page 90

Christmas tree page 90

Reindeer page 92

Gingerbread man page 93

Christmas ornaments page 91

Stockings page 92

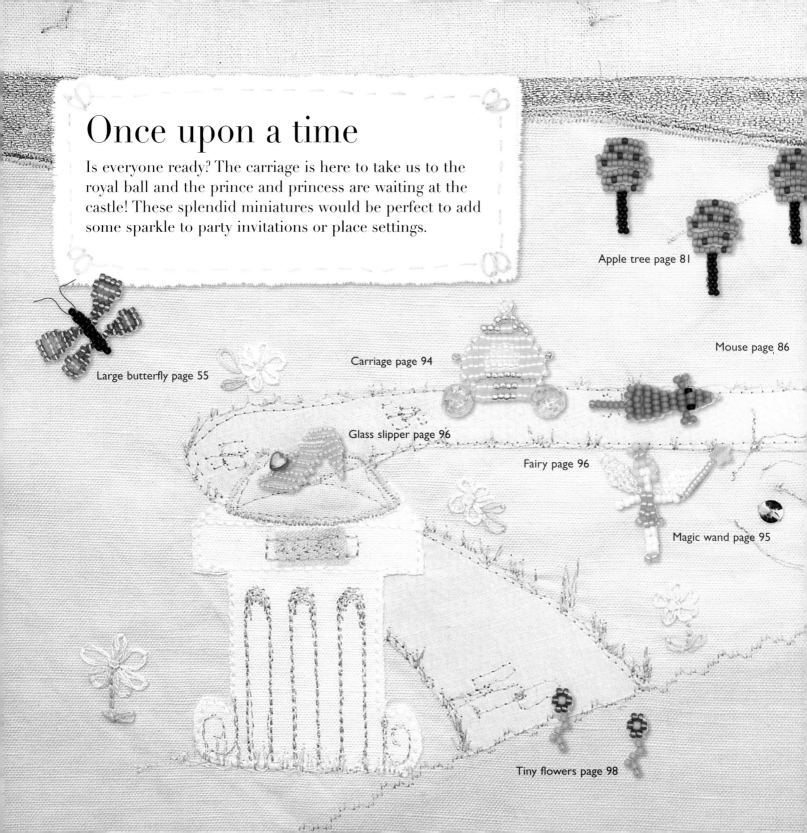

Once upon a time

Is everyone ready? The carriage is here to take us to the royal ball and the prince and princess are waiting at the castle! These splendid miniatures would be perfect to add some sparkle to party invitations or place settings.

Apple tree page 81

Mouse page 86

Large butterfly page 55

Carriage page 94

Glass slipper page 96

Fairy page 96

Magic wand page 95

Tiny flowers page 98

Castle page 95

Crown page 98

Prince page 97

Princess page 97

Simple butterfly page 55

Flower page 101

Be my Valentine

Have you been bitten by the love bug? Show someone how much you care with a box of charming little beaded chocolates. And who wouldn't want to receive a sweet love letter from a secret admirer? These charms make wonderful little adornments for Valentine cards.

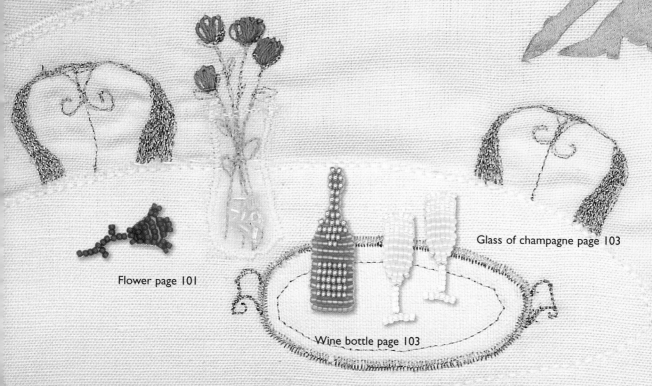

Love bugs page 101

Flower page 101

Wine bottle page 103

Glass of champagne page 103

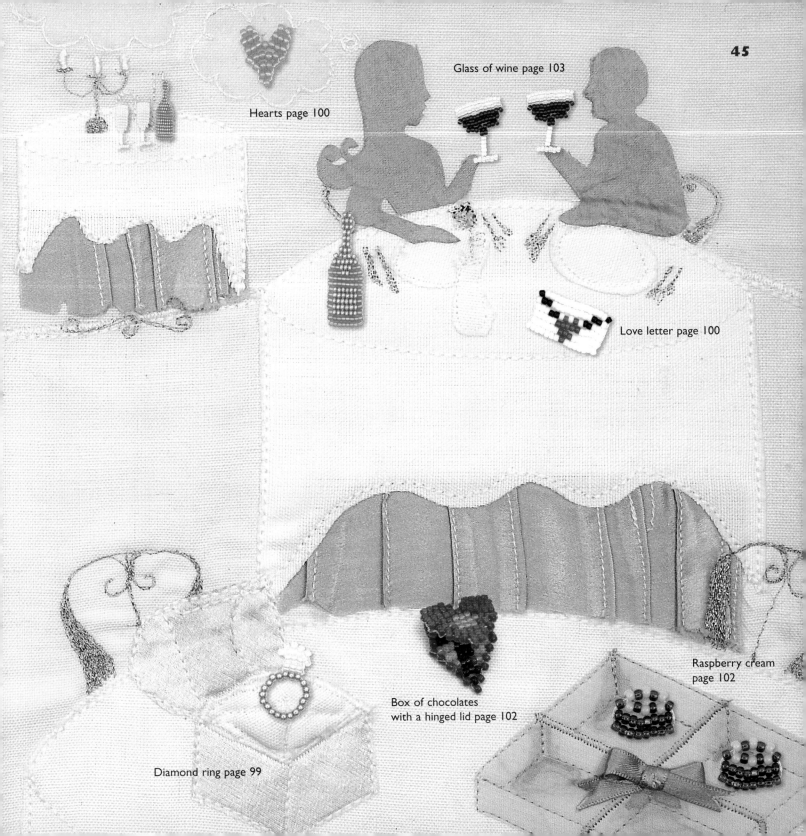

Hearts page 100

Glass of wine page 103

Love letter page 100

Diamond ring page 99

Box of chocolates
with a hinged lid page 102

Raspberry cream
page 102

Wonderland tea party

Happy Birthday! Or is it your unbirthday? Join Alice and friends for a slice of cake and a cup of tea to celebrate. There are cupcakes, tiny candles, and presents to enjoy, but make sure you don't eat the toadstools!

Balloons page 105

Teacup page 107

Candle page

Mad Hatter's cake page 105

Toadstool page 83

Cupcakes page 78

Cat page 85

Alice page 104

Party hats page 106

Presents page 106

Mouse page 86

Rabbit page 88

Teapot page 107

Tiny flowers page 98

Hearts page 100

Around the world

Pack your suitcase and get ready for an adventure. It's time to travel the world with this collection of treasures from near and far. These delightful little charms are perfect for wishing someone "Bon Voyage" or decorating a vacation scrapbook page.

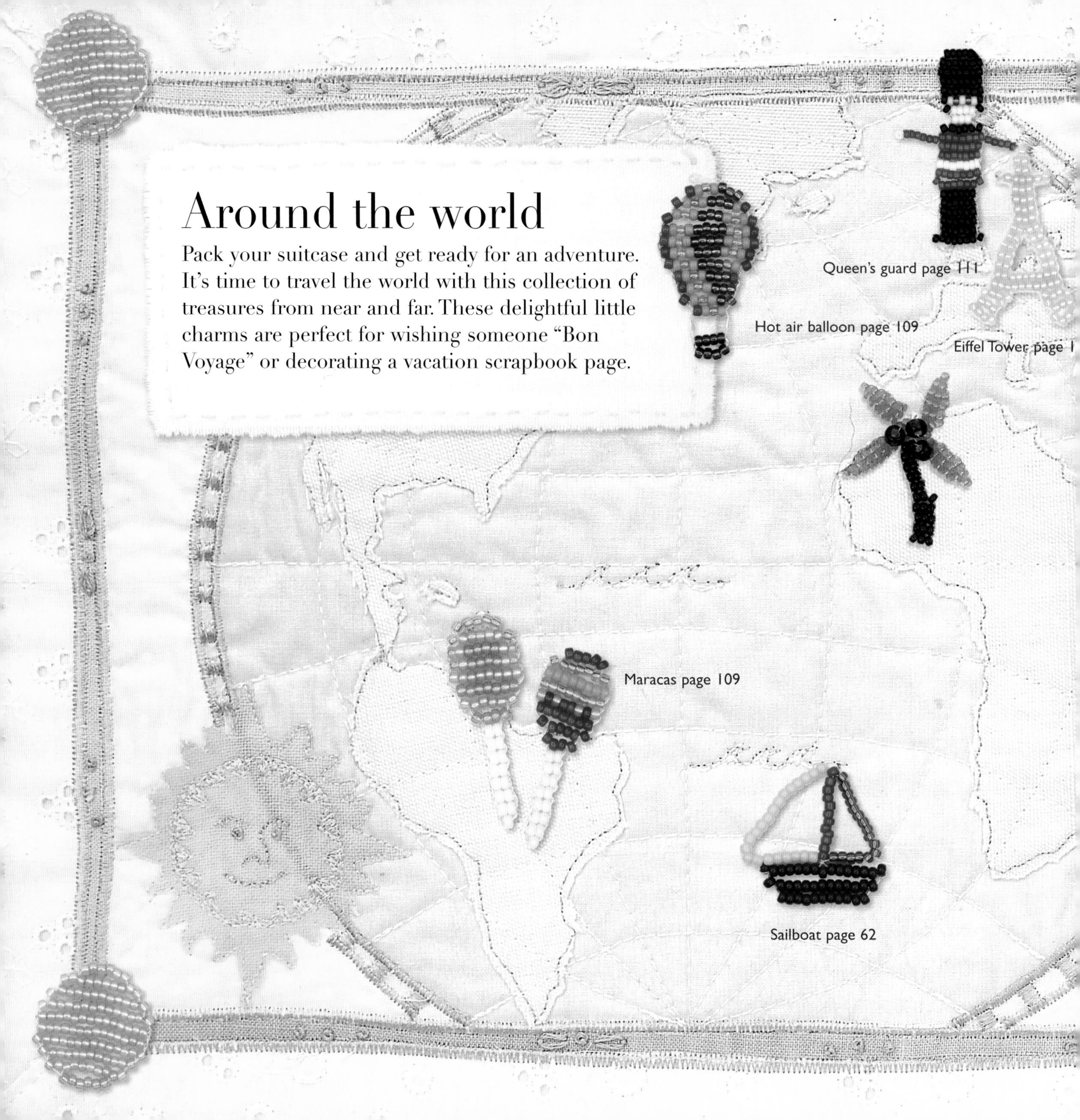

Queen's guard page 111

Hot air balloon page 109

Eiffel Tower page 1

Maracas page 109

Sailboat page 62

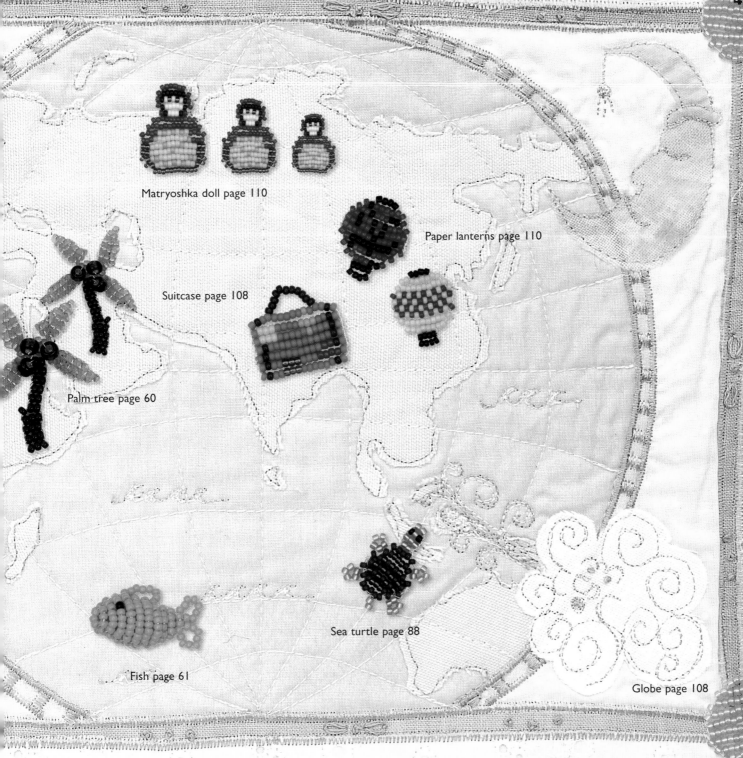

Matryoshka doll page 110

Paper lanterns page 110

Suitcase page 108

Palm tree page 60

Sea turtle page 88

Fish page 61

Globe page 108

Section 3:
Beading patterns

Bugs' world

Make your way through this chapter and discover how to bead up these weird and wonderful creatures:

1 Ant
2 Bee
3 Beetle
4 Dragonfly
5 Damselfly
6 Simple butterfly
7 Large butterfly
8 Monarch butterfly
9 Ladybug
10 Caterpillar
11 Spider

Ant

Tiny little ants always like to come along on picnics! Now you can make up several of your own to use on summer cards and scrapbook pages.

Easy

Bead store
● 41 black beads

You will need
• Basic tool kit
• 30 gauge (0.25mm) black and silver wire

Beading how to
To make the ant, use the basic assembly and adding wire appendages techniques on pages 18–21 and follow the wire path on the diagram.

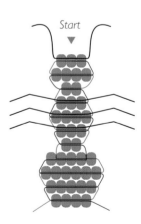

Key for the patterns: Blue is the left-hand end of the wire

2 Bee

Busy bees add a bit of fun to springtime jewelry and other craft projects. They would look adorable resting atop a beaded flower.

Easy

Bead store
- ● 22 black beads
- ○ 22 crystal iridescent beads
- ● 13 yellow beads

You will need
- Basic tool kit
- 30 gauge (0.25mm) silver wire

Beading how to
To make the bee, use the basic assembly techniques on pages 18–21 and follow the wire path on the diagram.

Start

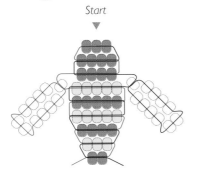

3 Beetle

There are many different kinds of beetles in the world. This beaded version would make a delightful addition to your beaded garden.

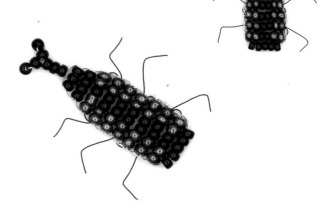

Easy

Bead store
- ● 32 black beads
- ● 28 iridescent dark green beads

You will need
- Basic tool kit
- 30 gauge (0.25mm) black and silver wire

Beading how to
To make the beetle, use the basic assembly and adding wire appendages techniques on pages 18–21 and follow the wire path on the diagram.

Start

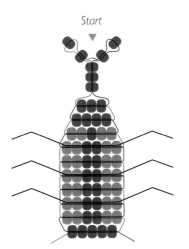

● **Red is the right-hand end of the wire**

4 Dragonfly

Dragonflies love to soar over pools and ponds, with their shimmering, iridescent wings glittering in the sunlight. Your beaded dragonflies will be just as beautiful using lovely iridescent beads.

Easy

Bead store

BLUE DRAGONFLY
- ● 14 black beads
- ● 36 iridescent blue beads

You will need
- Basic tool kit
- 30 gauge (0.25mm) silver wire

Beading how to
To make the dragonfly, use the basic assembly techniques on pages 18–21 and follow the wire path on the diagram.

Start

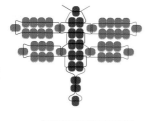

PURPLE DRAGONFLY
- ● 14 black beads
- ● 36 iridescent purple beads

5 Damselfly

It is such fun to watch these little beauties flitting around over ponds on a warm summer day! Now you can add this gorgeous little creature to all sorts of projects!

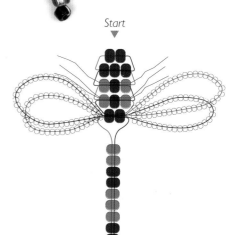

Easy

Bead store

DAMSELFLY
- ○ 150 iridescent clear beads
- ● 11 x 6/0 silver-lined blue beads
- ● 15 x 6/0 black beads

You will need
- Basic tool kit
- 28 gauge (0.3mm) silver wire

Beading how to
To make the damselfly, use the basic assembly and adding wire appendages techniques on pages 18–21 and follow the wire path on the diagram.

Start

Key for the patterns: Blue is the left-hand end of the wire ● Red is the right-hand end of the wire

6 Simple butterfly

These little butterflies are easy to work up. You can make them in every color for everyone you know!

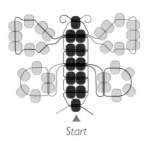

Easy
Bead store
- ● 12 black beads
- ○ 28 pink beads

You will need
- Basic tool kit
- 30 gauge (0.25mm) silver wire

Beading how to
To make the simple butterfly, use the basic assembly techniques on pages 18–21 and follow the wire path on the diagram.

Start

TIP
After beading the entire butterfly, make a couple of extra passes back through the top beads with the wire, making sure to come out on each side of the black top "head" bead. Trim each wire to about ½in (12mm). Use round-nose pliers to curl the extra wire to make the antenna.

7 Large butterfly

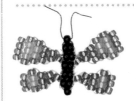

This large butterfly can be worked up in an endless variety of color combinations. They look beautiful used as pins and brooches.

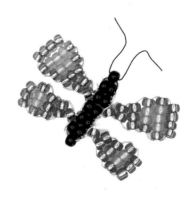

Intermediate
Bead store
- ● 12 black beads
- ● 50 purple beads
- ● 14 pink beads

You will need
- Basic tool kit
- 30 gauge (0.25mm) black and silver wire

Beading how to
To make the large butterly, use the basic assembly and adding wire appendages techniques on pages 18–21 and follow the wire path on the diagram.

Start
▼

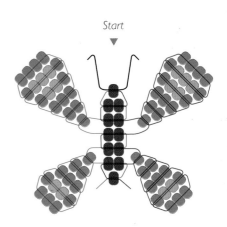

8 Monarch butterfly

Monarch butterflies love to flit and fly among flowers, lilacs and goldenrods being their favorites. This beaded monarch will be just as happy perched on a lapel or hat.

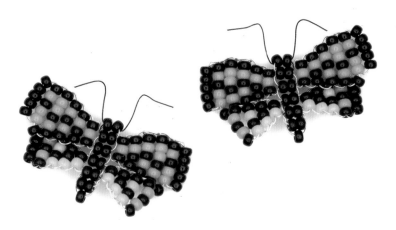

Intermediate
Bead store
- ● 75 black beads
- ● 24 orange beads
- ○ 8 yellow beads

You will need
- Basic tool kit
- 30 gauge (0.25mm) black and silver wire

Beading how to
Use the basic assembly and adding wire appendages techniques on pages 18–21 and follow the wire path on the diagram.

1 Bead the body as usual.

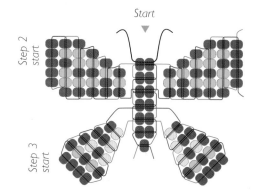

Start

Step 2 start

Step 3 start

2 Bead the top left wing as shown in the pattern. Then string the excess wire into the body as shown. Continue beading the top right wing.

3 Repeat for the bottom set of wings.

4 Secure the extra wire and trim the ends as usual.

9 Ladybug

Tradition states that a person's wish will be granted if a ladybug lands on them. What fun to create a whole collection of ladybugs to remind us of our wishes.

Easy
Bead store
- ● 9 black beads
- ● 13 red beads

You will need
- Basic tool kit
- 30 gauge (0.25mm) black and silver wire

Beading how to
To make the ladybug, use the basic assembly and adding wire appendages techniques on pages 18–21 and follow the wire path on the diagram.

Start

Key for the patterns: Blue is the left-hand end of the wire ● **Red is the right-hand end of the wire**

10 Caterpillar

Here is a bright and colorful little caterpillar that would be right at home in a nature-themed shadow box.

Intermediate

Bead store

- 49 lime green beads
- 18 yellow beads
- 11 red beads
- 2 black beads

You will need
- Basic tool kit
- 30 gauge (0.25mm) silver wire

Beading how to

To make the caterpillar, use the basic assembly techniques on pages 18–21 and follow the wire path on the diagram.

Start

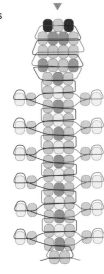

11 Spider

Here is a spider that you wouldn't mind having as a visitor! The finished charm makes a perfect little pendant.

Easy

Bead store

- 120 black beads
- 2 large black speckled glass beads

You will need
- 2in (5cm) headpin
- Round-nose pliers
- 30 gauge (0.25mm) silver wire

Beading how to

To make the spider, use the basic assembly techniques on pages 18–21 and follow the wire path on the diagram.

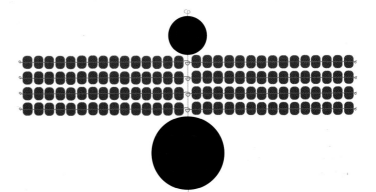

At the beach

This chapter will show you how you can put together all of these beach-themed charms:

12 Crab

Crabs love to burrow in tunnels at the beach. Luckily, you can keep your beaded ones out for everyone to see and enjoy.

Intermediate
Bead store
- 115 red beads
- 10 black beads

You will need
- Basic tool kit
- 30 gauge (0.25mm) silver wire

Beading how to
To make the crab, use the basic assembly techniques on pages 18–21 and follow the wire path on the diagram.

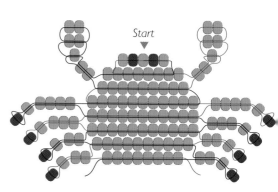

Start

Key for the patterns: Blue is the left-hand end of the wire

13 Starfish

These beautiful creatures are at home in the ocean. This beaded starfish would be at home as earrings or a pendant during a visit to the beach.

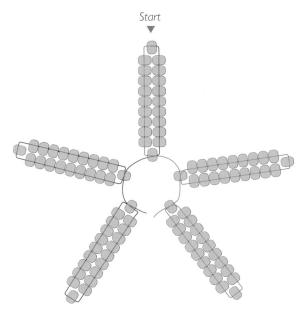

Easy

Bead store

● 100 coral beads

You will need
• Basic tool kit
• 30 gauge (0.25mm) silver wire

Beading how to
To make the starfish, use the basic assembly techniques on pages 18–21 and follow the wire path on the diagram.

Start ▼

14 Seashell

Seashells are often called "gifts from the sea." A bracelet filled with these beaded shells would be a perfect gift for the ocean enthusiast!

Easy

Bead store

○ 52 sandy beige beads
● 44 dark light brown beads

You will need
• Basic tool kit
• 30 gauge (0.25mm) silver wire

Beading how to
To make the seashell, use the basic assembly techniques on pages 18–21 and follow the wire path on the diagram.

Start ▼

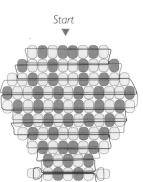

● **Red is the right-hand end of the wire**

15 Lighthouse

As beacons in the night, lighthouses serve an important purpose, as well as dotting the coastline with beautiful buildings for everyone to admire.

Easy

Bead store
- ● 40 red beads
- ● 35 black beads
- ○ 36 white beads
- ● 12 yellow beads

You will need
- Basic tool kit
- 30 gauge (0.25mm) silver wire

Beading how to
To make the lighthouse, use the basic assembly techniques on pages 18–21 and follow the wire path on the diagram.

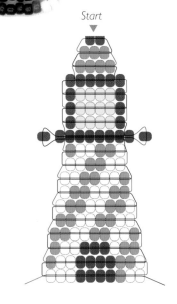

Start

16 Palm tree

Palm trees provide shade, produce coconuts, and lend a tropical feel no matter where they are. Little beaded versions are perfect for tropical craft projects.

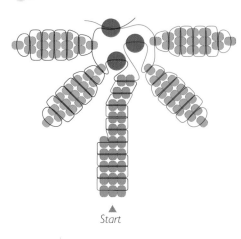

Intermediate

Bead store
- ● 60 green beads
- ● 25 brown beads
- ● 3 x 4mm round brown glass beads

You will need
- Basic tool kit
- 30 gauge (0.25mm) silver wire

Beading how to
To make the palm tree, use the basic assembly techniques on pages 18–21 and follow the wire path on the diagram.

Start

Key for the patterns: Blue is the left-hand end of the wire ● Red is the right-hand end of the wire

17 Fish

Everyone will want to catch one of these little fish. A whole beaded school of fish would be the perfect addition to a day at the beach!

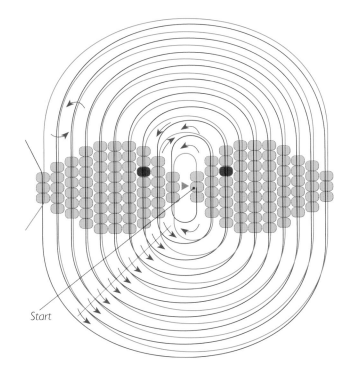

Challenging

Bead store

- 154 orange beads
- 2 black beads

You will need
- Basic tool kit
- 30 gauge (0.25mm) silver wire

Start

Beading how to

Use the basic assembly techniques on pages 18–21 and follow the wire path on the diagram.

1 Bead the body of the fish.

2 Add the top fin and tail fins by stringing those beads onto wire and weaving it into the body of the fish. You should end up with a 3-D charm.

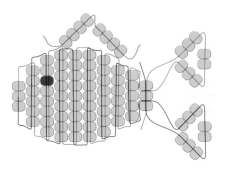

18 Sailboat

How fun to watch sailboats gliding over the water, the wind in their sails as they move smoothly along. Beaded sailboats will look fun on beach cards and scrapbook pages.

Easy

Bead store

- 39 brown beads
- 21 yellow beads
- 16 blue beads
- 12 red beads

You will need

- Basic tool kit
- 30 gauge (0.25mm) silver wire

Beading how to

To make the sailboat, use the basic assembly techniques on pages 18–21 and follow the wire path on the diagram.

▲ *Start*

19 Shovel and pail

These are the two most important tools for building sandcastles at the beach. You can't go on vacation without these!

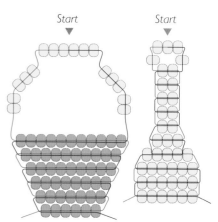

Easy

Bead store

PAIL

- 51 red beads
- 16 yellow beads

SHOVEL

- 41 yellow beads

You will need

- Basic tool kit
- 30 gauge (0.25mm) silver wire

Beading how to

To make the shovel and pail, use the basic assembly techniques on pages 18–21 and follow the wire path on the diagram.

Start ▼   *Start* ▼

Key for the patterns: Blue is the left-hand end of the wire ● Red is the right-hand end of the wire

20 Flip-flops

Flip-flops are the ultimate symbol of summer at the beach. Make up a few pairs to match all your summer outfits!

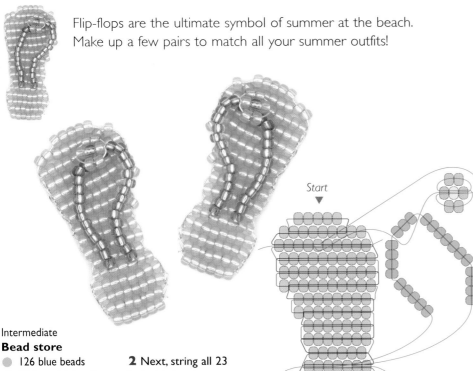

Start ▼

Intermediate

Bead store
- ● 126 blue beads
- ● 30 hot pink beads
- ● 6 lime green beads
- ○ 1 yellow bead

You will need
- Basic tool kit
- 30 gauge (0.25mm) silver wire

Beading how to
Use the basic assembly techniques on pages 18–21 and follow the wire path on the diagram.

1 Assemble the blue flip-flop base using basic assembly techniques.

2 Next, string all 23 hot pink beads on a separate wire. Insert each end of the wire into the fifth row from the bottom of the flip-flop base, as pictured right. Secure the ends.

3 Make a small flower using the lime green and yellow beads. Do not trim the extra wire.

4 Using the extra wire from the flower, secure the top of the pink beaded wire to the flip-flop base. Secure the extra wire and trim the ends as usual.

21 Umbrella

One of the most familiar sights at the beach is seeing the coastline scattered with big beach umbrellas. These beaded umbrellas are a fun way to add a touch of the beach to your craft projects.

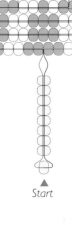

Easy

Bead store
- ● 30 red beads
- ○ 30 white beads
- ● 9 gray beads

You will need
- Basic tool kit
- 30 gauge (0.25mm) silver wire

Beading how to
To make the umbrella, use the basic assembly techniques on pages 18–21 and follow the wire path on the diagram.

▲ *Start*

At the diner

Explore this chapter and select from these patterns and bead up your favorite treat:

22 Battenberg cake

Battenberg cake is a popular British treat, served on special holidays or with tea. These little beaded slices would make fun, unique jewelry for the tea lover.

Easy

Bead store

PINK BATTENBERG
- 24 pink beads
- 24 yellow beads
- 32 cream beads

You will need
- Basic tool kit
- 30 gauge (0.25mm) silver wire

Beading how to
To make the battenberg cake slice, use the basic assembly techniques on pages 18–21 and follow the wire path on the diagram.

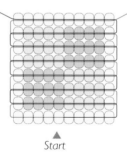

▲
Start

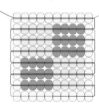

BROWN BATTENBERG
- 24 brown beads
- 24 yellow beads
- 32 cream beads

Key for the patterns: Blue is the left-hand end of the wire

23 Bubble tea

Bubble tea is a sweet drink that originated in Asia. Small tapioca pearls, or "boba," are added to the mixture, creating visual interest and a delicious surprise!

Easy
Bead store
- 54 pink beads
- ○ 8 clear beads
- 8 green beads
- ● 5 black beads

You will need
- Basic tool kit
- 30 gauge (0.25mm) silver wire

Beading how to
To make the bubble tea, use the basic assembly techniques on pages 18–21 and follow the wire path on the diagram.

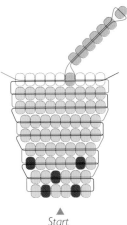

Start

24 Cheeseburger

A version of the traditional cheeseburger can be found almost anywhere. No matter how you serve them, they are always delicious. You can make up this beaded version with any toppings you like.

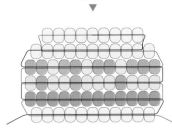

Start

Easy
Bead store
- 31 tan beads
- ● 12 brown beads
- 9 orange beads
- ● 6 red beads
- 6 green beads
- 3 yellow beads

You will need
- Basic tool kit
- 30 gauge (0.25mm) silver wire

Beading how to
To make the cheeseburger, use the basic assembly techniques on pages 18–21 and follow the wire path on the diagram.

● **Red is the right-hand end of the wire**

25 Cherries

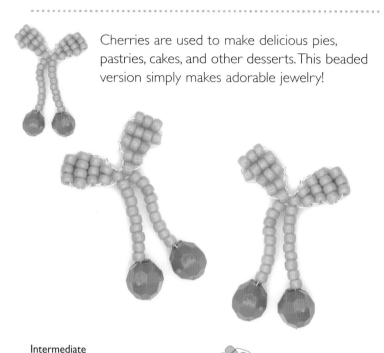

Cherries are used to make delicious pies, pastries, cakes, and other desserts. This beaded version simply makes adorable jewelry!

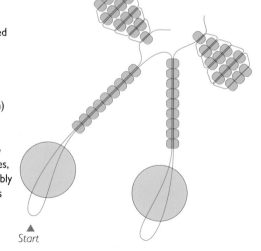

Intermediate
Bead store
● 44 green beads
● 2 x 6mm faceted red beads

You will need
• Basic tool kit
• 30 gauge (0.25mm) silver wire

Beading how to
To make the cherries, use the basic assembly techniques on pages 18–21 and follow the wire path on the diagram.

Start

26 Parfaits

Parfaits can be made with a wide variety of fruit, creams, and syrups. The only limit to these beaded versions is your imagination!

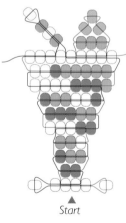
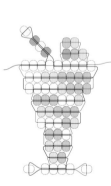

Easy
Bead store
BERRIES AND CREAM
○ 15 crystal beads
○ 12 white beads
● 17 red beads
● 14 blue beads
○ 2 cream beads
● 2 brown beads
● 3 green beads

You will need
• Basic tool kit
• 30 gauge (0.25mm) silver wire

Beading how to
To make the parfaits, use the basic assembly techniques on pages

Start

18–21 and follow the wire path on the diagram.

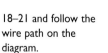

PEACHES AND CREAM
○ 15 crystal beads
○ 12 white beads
● 1 red bead
○ 2 cream beads
● 2 brown beads
● 20 orange beads
● 12 yellow beads

27 Pizza slice

Pizza is an incredibly versatile food. There are so many toppings—ranging from savory to sweet—that can be added. This beaded version is topped with all the traditional favorites.

Easy
Bead store
- 26 brown beads
- 15 red beads
- 10 green beads
- 26 cream beads

You will need
- Basic tool kit
- 30 gauge (0.25mm) silver wire

Beading how to
To make the pizza slice, use the basic assembly techniques on pages 18–21 and follow the wire path on the diagram.

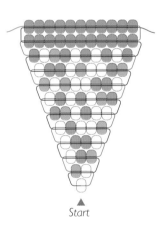

Start

TIP
Fold up the last row of crust for a fun three-dimensional effect!

28 Sushi roll slices

Delicious rice and fillings wrapped in edible seaweed make a yummy snack, as well as offer an appealing presentation. These beaded slices look just as appetizing when used in jewelry and cards!

Easy
Bead store
EGG
- 16 black beads
- ○ 16 white beads
- 2 orange beads
- 2 yellow beads

You will need
- Basic tool kit
- 30 gauge (0.25mm) silver wire

Beading how to
To make the sushi roll slices, use the basic assembly techniques on pages 18–21 and follow the wire path on the diagram.

Start

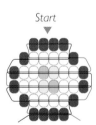

CUCUMBER
- 16 black beads
- ○ 16 white beads
- 2 dark green beads
- 2 light green beads

SHRIMP
- 16 black beads
- ○ 16 white beads
- 2 orange beads
- 1 green bead
- 1 red bead

29 Popsicles

30 Bananas

Delicious frozen popsicles are a wonderful treat on a hot day. Make up all your favorite flavors to include on a charm bracelet!

These bananas work up quickly and would look simply adorable paired with the little beaded monkey on page 85!

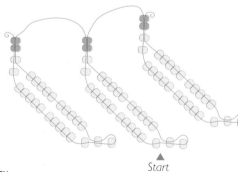

Easy
Bead store
DOUBLE POPSICLE
● 62 pink beads
○ 16 cream beads

SMALL POPSICLE
○ 31 green, red, or yellow beads
○ 8 cream beads

You will need
• Basic tool kit
• 30 gauge (0.25mm) silver wire

Beading how to
To make the small popsicle and the double popsicle, use the basic assembly techniques on pages 18–21 and follow the wire path on the diagram.

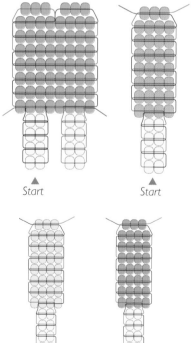

▲
Start

▲
Start

Easy
Bead store
BANANAS
○ 63 yellow beads
● 6 brown beads

You will need
• Basic tool kit
• 30 gauge (0.25mm) silver wire

▲
Start

Beading how to
To make the bananas, use the basic assembly techniques on pages 18–21 and follow the wire path on the diagram.

Key for the patterns: Blue is the left-hand end of the wire ● Red is the right-hand end of the wire

In the garden

Flick through this chapter and choose from these intricate floral patterns to create a wonderful beaded bouquet:

31 Clematis

The clematis symbolizes ingenuity. Perhaps this is due to the climbing, moving nature of this hardy flower.

Intermediate

Bead store

(There may be some extra pink and purple beads; this amount assures enough for all petals no matter which color you choose for each petal)

- ● 230 pink beads
- ○ 231 crystal beads
- ○ 28 white beads
- ● 8 yellow beads

You will need
- Basic tool kit
- 30 gauge (0.25mm) silver wire

Beading how to
To make the clematis, using the techniques on pages 18–23, follow the wire path on the diagram to make the flower components and then assemble.

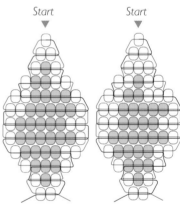

Start   *Start*

Petal x 4   Petal x 3

Start ▶

Stamens x 1

32 Dog rose

Pink dog roses symbolize perfect happiness. Their blooms make beautiful decorations, and these beaded blossoms will make delightful brooches to decorate an outfit.

Intermediate

Bead store
- ● 200 pink beads
- ○ 220 white beads
- ● 67 yellow beads

You will need
- Basic tool kit
- 30 gauge (0.25mm) silver wire

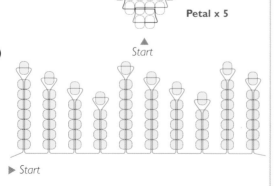

Petal x 5

▲ *Start*

▶ *Start*

Beading how to
To make the dog rose, use the techniques on pages 18–23 and follow the wire path on the diagram to make the flower components and then assemble.

33 Tulip

Different colors of tulips symbolize different things. Yellow tulips symbolize cheerful thoughts. This beaded tulip is sure to bring cheerful thoughts to all those who see it.

Easy

Bead store
- ● 160 red beads
- ○ 269 yellow beads
- ● 90 orange beads
- ● 18 brown beads

You will need
- Basic tool kit
- 30 gauge (0.25mm) silver wire

Beading how to
To make the tulip, use the techniques on pages 18–23 and follow the wire path on the diagram to make the flower components and then assemble.

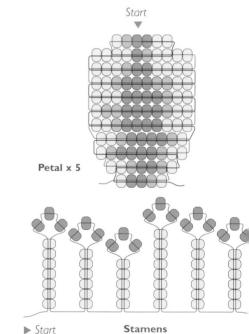

Start ▼

Petal x 5

▶ *Start*   **Stamens**

Key for the patterns: Blue is the left-hand end of the wire ● Red is the right-hand end of the wire

34 Daisy

White daisies have long been a symbol of innocence and purity; however, you can make up a whole bouquet of beaded daisies in any colors you wish.

Easy
Bead store
○ 250 white beads
● 27 yellow beads

You will need
• Basic tool kit
• 30 gauge (0.25mm) silver wire

Beading how to
Use the basic assembly and flower assembly techniques on pages 18–23 and follow the wire path on the diagram.

1 String 25 white beads onto the wire. Pass the wire back through the first bead strung.

2 Continue with this pattern until you have completed 10 petals.

3 Secure any extra wire and trim the ends as usual.

4 Attach the center.

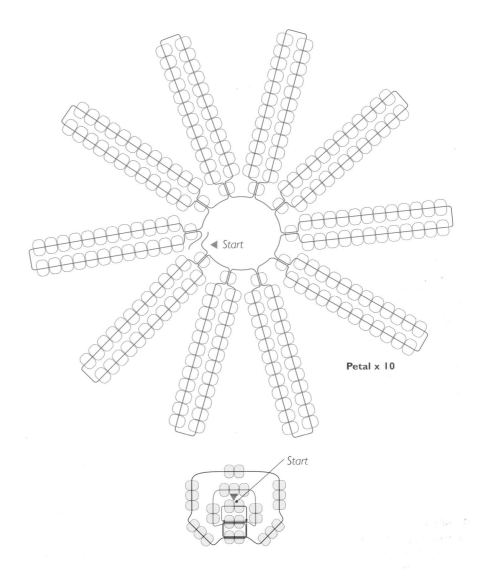

Start

Petal x 10

Start

35 Fuchsia

Fuchsia flowers are undoubtedly one of the most unique to be found. Their bright coloring attracts hummingbirds. The beaded blooms make a beautiful pendant.

Challenging

Bead store
- 133 magenta beads
- 90 purple beads
- 36 green beads
- ○ 9 white beads

You will need
- Basic tool kit
- 30 gauge (0.25mm) silver wire
- 36 gauge (0.13mm) silver wire

Beading how to

1 Using the basic assembly technique on pages 18–23, assemble four sepals, starting at the top.

2 Assemble two tubes and, before securing and trimming the ends, attach two sepals to each tube as in the diagram.

3 Next, connect the two tubes along their sides, using 36-gauge wire.

4 Assemble three petals. String them together and attach beneath the sepals, weaving in the extra wire from connecting the three petals.

5 Assemble the pistil and stamens and attach those in the same way as the three petals.

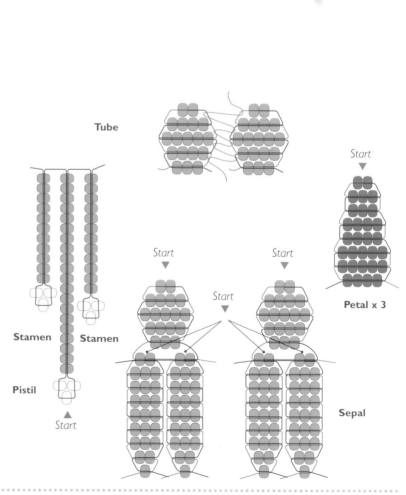

Tube

Start

Petal x 3

Start

Start

Start

Stamen   Stamen

Pistil

Start

Sepal

Key for the patterns: Blue is the left-hand end of the wire ● Red is the right-hand end of the wire

36 Morning glory

Morning glories symbolize affection. They open only in the morning and last for just a single day—but you can create a beaded version to enjoy for much longer.

Intermediate
Bead store
- 335 blue beads
- ○ 45 white beads
- 4 yellow beads

You will need
- Basic tool kit
- 30 gauge (0.25mm) silver wire

Petal x 5

Start

Beading how to

1 Assemble the first petal using the basic assembly techniques on pages 18–23.

2 For each remaining petal, you will go through the wire on the last petal in the corresponding rows

before continuing on with the beaded rows.

3 On the final petal, the wire on each side will go through the wires on the edge of the first petal, and the wires on the petal just completed.

4 After all petals are assembled, string four yellow beads and attach to the center of the flower.

37 Poppy

Poppies are associated with beauty, magic, and eternal life. A whole bouquet of beaded poppies would make a beautiful centerpiece for any occasion!

Easy
Bead store
- 495 red beads
- ● 55 black beads

You will need
- Basic tool kit
- 30 gauge (0.25mm) silver wire

Start

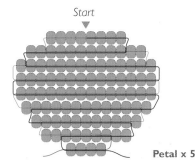

Petal x 5

Beading how to
To make the poppy, use the basic assembly and flower assembly techniques on pages 18–23 and follow the wire path on the diagram.

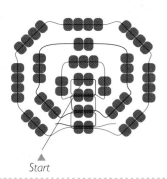

Start

38 Pansy

The French have a custom of giving brides a bouquet of pansies on their wedding day. A colorful bouquet of beaded pansies would make a unique gift that will last a lifetime!

Start

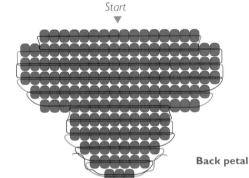

Back petal

Easy

Bead store
- 261 purple beads
- 36 yellow beads
- ○ 105 white beads

You will need
- Basic tool kit
- 30 gauge (0.25mm) silver wire

Beading how to
To make the pansy, use the techniques on pages 18–23 and follow the wire path on the diagram to make the flower components and then assemble.

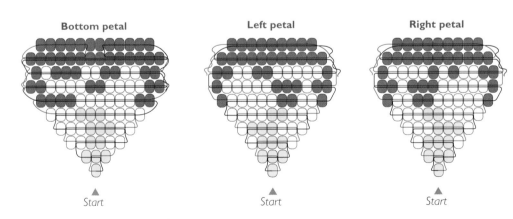

Bottom petal   Left petal   Right petal

Start   Start   Start

The bakery

Look through this treat-filled chapter and work up as many of these beaded delights as you want:

39 Dipped strawberries

These make a delicious addition to cards and jewelry! You can "dip" your strawberries in white or milk chocolate.

Easy
Bead store
MILK CHOCOLATE
- 39 red beads
- 25 green beads
- 16 brown beads

You will need
- Basic tool kit
- 30 gauge (0.25mm) silver wire

Beading how to
To make the chocolate-dipped strawberry, use the basic assembly and flower assembly techniques on pages 18–21, and follow the wire path on the diagram.

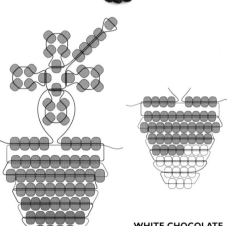

Start

WHITE CHOCOLATE
- 39 red beads
- 25 green beads
- ○ 16 white beads

40 Heart cookies

These sweet little heart cookies are adorable made using either a golden sugar-cookie base or a deep chocolate cookie base! Change colors to create customized icing and sprinkle patterns to make the perfect cookie for even the most particular gourmand!

Easy

Bead store

PINK SUGAR COOKIE
- 🔴 31 magenta beads
- ⚪ 24 creamy yellow beads
- ⚪ 8 white beads

CHOCOLATE COOKIE
- 🔴 24 dark brown beads
- ⚪ 31 white beads
- 🔴 4 red beads
- 🟡 4 pink beads

You will need
- Basic tool kit
- 30 gauge (0.25mm) silver wire

Beading how to
To make the heart cookies, use the basic assembly techniques on pages 18–21 and follow the wire path on the diagram.

▲ *Start*

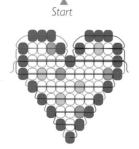

41 Macaroons

Parisian macaroons are a very special, delicious treat! Now you can "bake" up all your favorite flavors as little beaded miniatures to use for charms and jewelry!

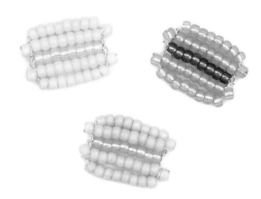

Easy

Bead store
- 🔴 36 lavender beads
- ⚪ 8 violet beads

You will need
- Basic tool kit
- 30 gauge (0.25mm) silver wire

Beading how to
To make the macaroon, use the basic assembly techniques on pages 18–21 and follow the wire path on the diagram.

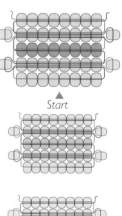

▲ *Start*

Key for the patterns: Blue is the left-hand end of the wire ● Red is the right-hand end of the wire

42 Petit fours

43 Ice cream cones

Petit fours are simple, tiny little cakes covered in glacé icing. Usually a small garnish, such as a rose or some leaves, is added to the top. These miniature versions will make a great addition to your beaded bakery!

This is an adorable design to use for all those summer projects! It's easy to customize your ice cream and toppings to your favorite flavors, too.

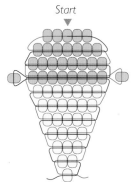

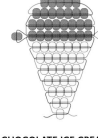

Easy

Bead store
- ⚪ 40 yellow beads
- 🟢 3 green beads

You will need
- Basic tool kit
- 30 gauge (0.25mm) silver wire

Beading how to
To make the petit fours, use the basic assembly techniques on pages 18–21, and follow the wire path on the diagram.

Start ▲

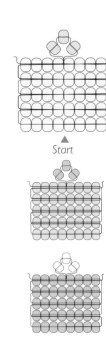

Easy

Bead store

STRAWBERRY ICE CREAM
- ⚪ 28 cream beads
- 🔴 30 pink beads

You will need
- Basic tool kit
- 30 gauge (0.25mm) silver wire

Beading how to
To make the ice-cream cones, use the basic assembly techniques on pages 18–21 and follow the wire path on the diagram.

Start ▼

VANILLA ICE CREAM WITH A CHERRY ON TOP
- ⚪ 28 cream beads
- ⚪ 29 white beads
- 🔴 1 x 4mm red crystal bicone

CHOCOLATE ICE CREAM
- ⚪ 28 cream beads
- ⚫ 30 brown beads

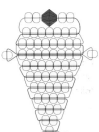

44 Éclair

This sweet miniature chocolate éclair design would look adorable combined with other cake charms on a bracelet.

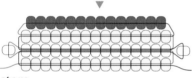

Start

Easy

Bead store
- ○ 30 cream beads
- ○ 17 white beads
- ● 14 brown beads

You will need
- Basic tool kit
- 30 gauge (0.25mm) silver wire

Beading how to
To make the éclair, use the basic assembly techniques on pages 18–21 and follow the wire path on the diagram.

45 Cupcakes

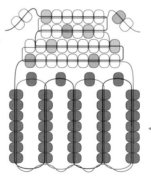

Cupcakes are very popular right now. Who could resist mounds of fluffy buttercream, resting atop moist delicious cake? These beaded versions look just as tasty, but without the mess!

Easy

Bead store

VANILLA BUTTERCREAM, CHOCOLATE CAKE, AND SPRINKLES
- ● 39 brown beads
- ○ 26 white beads
- ● 4 pink beads
- ● 4 blue beads

You will need
- Basic tool kit
- 30 gauge (0.25mm) silver wire

Beading how to
To make the cupcakes, use the basic assembly techniques on pages 18–21 and follow the wire path on the diagram.

◄ *Start*

CHOCOLATE BUTTERCREAM AND STRAWBERRY CAKE
- ● 39 pink beads
- ● 34 brown beads

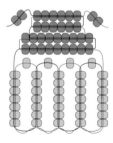

STRAWBERRY BUTTERCREAM AND VANILLA CAKE
- ● 34 pink beads
- ○ 39 cream beads

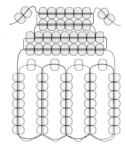

Key for the patterns: Blue is the left-hand end of the wire ● Red is the right-hand end of the wire

46 Party ring cookies

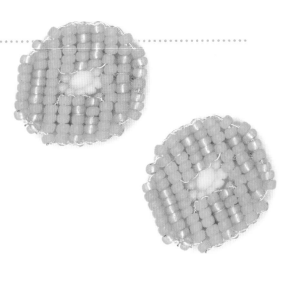

Party rings are a tasty British treat; a sweet cookie topped with colorful icing. These make beautiful charms and pendants.

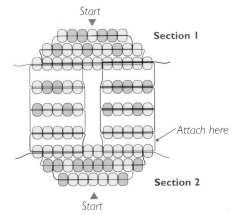

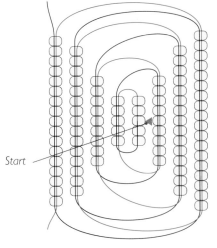

Challenging

Bead store
- 92 cream beads
- 62 yellow beads
- 26 pink beads

You will need
- Basic tool kit
- 30 gauge (0.25mm) silver wire
- 36 gauge (0.13mm) silver wire

Beading how to
To make the party ring cookie, use the basic assembly techniques on pages 18–21 and follow the wire path on the diagram.

1 Assemble the first section of the icing, and secure and trim the wire ends.

2 Assemble the second section of icing and attach it to the first section before securing and trimming the wire ends.

3 Assemble the bottom biscuit layer. Use 36 gauge (0.13mm) wire to attach the icing to the cookie.

Start

Section 1

Attach here

Section 2

Start

Start

Nature trail

This chapter has all sorts of woodland flora and fauna for you to choose from:

47 Deer

Deer are so quiet that you can sometimes miss them in the forest. Make sure that everyone can see your little beaded deer.

Easy

Bead store
- 76 brown beads
- 36 pink beads
- ○ 19 white beads
- ● 11 black beads

You will need
- Basic tool kit
- 30 gauge (0.25mm) silver wire

Beading how to
To make the deer, use the basic assembly techniques on pages 18–21. Assemble the head and ears separately. Do not secure and trim off the excess wire on the ears. Instead, use the extra wire to attach each ear to the head.

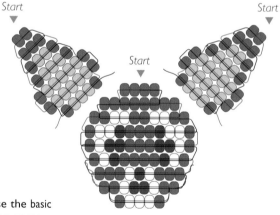

Start *Start*

Start

Key for the patterns: Blue is the left-hand end of the wire

48 Apple tree

You can build an entire orchard of little beaded apple trees for your animals and gnomes to play in! Use orange beads to create orange trees, or yellow beads for lemon trees.

Easy

Bead store
- 52 green beads
- 12 brown beads
- 8 red beads

You will need
- Basic tool kit
- 30 gauge (0.25mm) silver wire

Beading how to
To make the apple tree, use the basic assembly techniques on pages 18–21 and follow the wire path on the diagram.

Start ▼

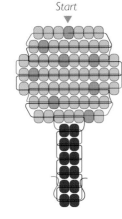

49 Acorns

Acorns are all over the ground in the woods. These little acorns will make delightful embellishments and charms for all your woodland-themed projects!

Easy

Bead store
- 12 green beads
- 16 brown beads
or
- 12 dark brown beads
- 16 light brown beads
or
- 12 light brown beads
- 16 dark brown beads

You will need
- Basic tool kit
- 30 gauge (0.25mm) silver wire

Beading how to
To make the acorns, use the basic assembly techniques on pages 18–21 and follow the wire path on the diagram.

Start ▲

50 Gnome

Little gnomes like to hide in the woods, but often come out to help travelers. Make sure everyone sees this cute little guy in all your projects.

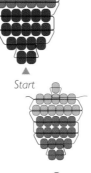

Easy

Bead store
- 55 light blue beads
- 21 red beads
- 18 peach beads
- O 22 white beads
- 2 blue beads
- ● 22 black beads
- 6 brown beads

You will need
- Basic tool kit
- 30 gauge (0.25mm) silver wire

Beading how to
To make the gnome, use the basic assembly techniques on pages 18–21 and follow the wire path on the diagram.

Start ▼

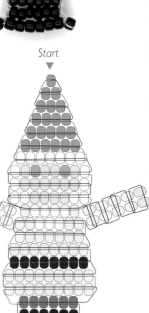

• **Red is the right-hand end of the wire**

51 Leaves

Make up these leaves in cool greens during the summer and warm shades of yellows, browns, and reds during the fall. They make a great addition to flower and fruit charms.

Easy

Bead store

GREEN LEAVES

- 48 light green beads
- 27 dark green beads

You will need

- Basic tool kit
- 30 gauge (0.25mm) silver wire

Beading how to

To make the leaves, use the basic assembly techniques on pages 18–21 and follow the wire path on the diagram.

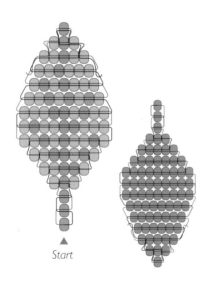

Start

BROWN LEAVES

- 75 brown beads

52 Owl

Owls are very much in style right now. This cute little beaded owl will make adorable jewelry or embellishments on cards or scrapbook pages.

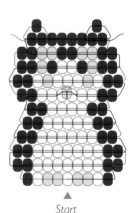

Easy

Bead store

- ● 50 brown beads
- ○ 45 white beads
- 13 yellow beads
- ● 2 black beads

You will need

- Basic tool kit
- 30 gauge (0.25mm) silver wire

Beading how to

To make the owl, use the basic assembly techniques on pages 18–21 and follow the wire path on the diagram. When adding the beads for the seventh row, add an extra yellow bead on

Start

one of the wires. This will rise above the rest of the row, making a little beak.

53 Toadstool

These little toadstools spring up everywhere! You can't have a walk through the woods without a few of these little guys.

Challenging

Bead store
- ● 70 red beads
- ○ 42 white beads

You will need
- Basic tool kit
- 30 gauge (0.25mm) silver wire

Beading how to

To make the toadstool, use the basic assembly techniques on pages 18–21 and follow the wire path on the diagram to make the cap. After the cap is finished, construct the stem and attach it to the top of the stem by weaving the extra wire into the cap. You should end up with a 3-D charm.

Start

Finished top

Start stem

54 Fox

The sly little fox is a master of trickery and deceit, but this beaded fox will make a fun little charm or pin!

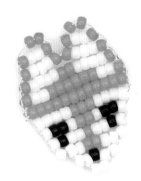 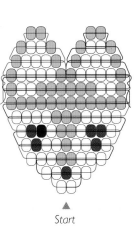

Easy

Bead store
- ● 44 orange beads
- ○ 52 white beads
- ● 7 black beads

You will need
- Basic tool kit
- 30 gauge (0.25mm) silver wire

Beading how to

To make the fox, use the basic assembly techniques on pages 18–21 and follow the wire path on the diagram.

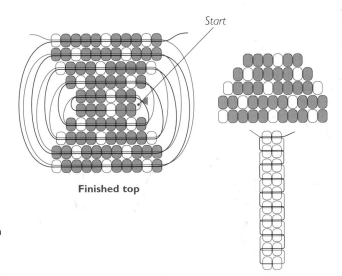

▲
Start

Animal crackers

Take your pick from these cute little critters and bead yourself a whole zoo:

55 Bear

This is one of the friendliest bears you will meet! He would love to be included in your camping and outdoor projects.

Easy
Bead store
● 66 brown beads
● 8 black beads

You will need
• Basic tool kit
• 30 gauge (0.25mm) silver wire

Beading how to
To make the bear, use the basic assembly techniques on pages 18–21 and follow the wire path on the diagram.

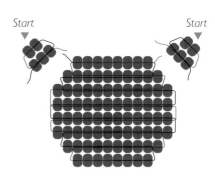

Start   *Start*

Start

Key for the patterns: **Blue is the left-hand end of the wire**

56 Cat

57 Monkey

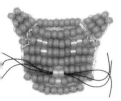

Curious cats are so much fun! This one would be at home on any pet-themed scrapbook page or charm bracelet.

Monkeys look so cute swinging around in the trees! These will look just as cute in all your jungle-themed projects.

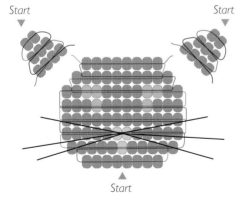

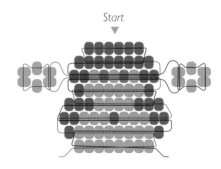

Easy

Bead store
- 94 gray beads
- 6 blue beads
- 3 pink beads

You will need
- Basic tool kit
- 30 gauge (0.25mm) black and silver wire

Beading how to
To make the cat, use the basic assembly and adding wire appendages techniques on pages 18–21 and follow the wire path on the diagram.

Start

Start

Start

Easy

Bead store
- 47 light brown beads
- 33 dark brown beads
- 2 black beads

You will need
- Basic tool kit
- 30 gauge (0.25mm) silver wire

Beading how to
To make the monkey, use the basic assembly techniques on pages 18–21 and follow the wire path on the diagram.

Start

● **Red is the right-hand end of the wire**

58 Mouse

These tiny mice are quick to bead up, and make adorable embellishments on all sorts of projects.

Easy
Bead store
- 52 gray beads
- 2 black beads
- 1 pink bead

You will need
- Basic tool kit
- 30 gauge (0.25mm) silver wire

Beading how to
To make the mouse, use the basic assembly techniques on pages 18–21 and follow the wire path on the diagram.

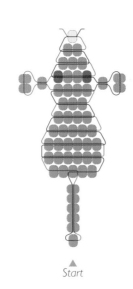

▲ *Start*

59 Penguin

Waddling around in a tiny tuxedo, this cute little penguin is perfect for anyone who has a soft spot for Antarctic animals!

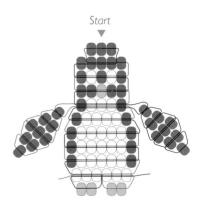

Easy
Bead store
- 43 black beads
- ○ 30 white beads
- 5 orange beads

You will need
- Basic tool kit
- 30 gauge (0.25mm) silver wire

Beading how to
To make the penguin, use the basic assembly techniques on pages 18–21 and follow the wire path on the diagram.

Start ▼

60 Pig

Pink pigs love playing in the mud! This one will certainly love playing around in your jewelry designs as well!

Easy

Bead store
- 88 pink beads
- 12 dark pink beads
- 2 black beads

You will need
- Basic tool kit
- 30 gauge (0.25mm) silver wire

Beading how to
To make the pig, use the basic assembly techniques on pages 18–21 and follow the wire path on the diagram.

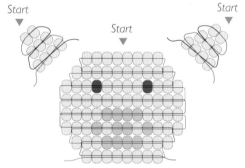

61 Dog

This little puppy will quickly charm his way into your heart! He would make a great addition to any little boy's birthday card or gift tag.

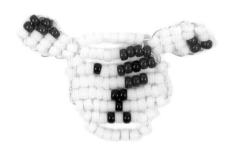

Easy

Bead store
- O 87 white beads
- 19 brown beads
- 7 black beads

You will need
- Basic tool kit
- 30 gauge (0.25mm) silver wire

Beading how to
To make the dog, use the basic assembly techniques on pages 18–21 and follow the wire path on the diagram.

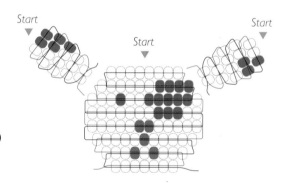

62 Rabbit

You have to be quick to catch this speedy little rabbit! So cute for Easter-themed cards and scrapbook pages.

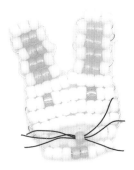

Easy

Bead store
- ○ 75 white beads
- ● 2 blue beads
- ● 19 pink beads

You will need
- Basic tool kit
- 30 gauge (0.25mm) black and silver wire

Beading how to
To make the rabbit, use the basic assembly and adding wire appendages techniques on pages 18–21 and follow the wire path on the diagram.

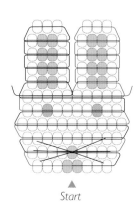

Start

63 Sea turtle

Surf's up! This endearing turtle feels right at home in the water. He would also love to be in any of your ocean-themed projects.

Easy

Bead store
- ● 30 green beads
- ● 20 light brown beads
- ● 40 dark brown beads
- ● 2 black beads

You will need
- Basic tool kit
- 30 gauge (0.25mm) silver wire

Beading how to
To make the sea turtle, use the basic assembly techniques on pages 18–21 and follow the wire path on the diagram.

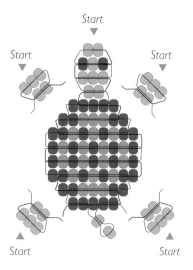

Start

Start   *Start*

Start   *Start*

Key for the patterns: Blue is the left-hand end of the wire ● Red is the right-hand end of the wire

Happy holidays

Celebrate the holidays by creating some of these festive charms:

64 Snowman

What a delightful snowman! The best part about this little beaded version is that he will never melt.

Easy

Bead store
- ○ 70 white beads
- ● 25 black beads
- 5 red beads
- 4 green beads
- 1 orange beads

You will need
- Basic tool kit
- 30 gauge (0.25mm) silver wire

Beading how to
To make the snowman, use the basic assembly techniques on pages 18–21 and follow the wire path on the diagram.

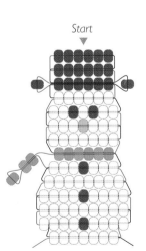

Start

65 Christmas tree

Picking out a Christmas tree during the holidays is so much fun! And now you can bead up as many as you like to include in all your Christmas projects!

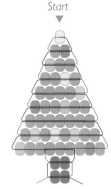

Easy

Bead store
- 31 green beads
- 3 red beads
- 3 orange beads
- 3 yellow beads
- 3 blue beads
- 3 pink beads
- 4 brown beads

You will need
- Basic tool kit
- 30 gauge (0.25mm) silver wire

Beading how to
To make the Christmas tree, use the basic assembly techniques on pages 18–21 and follow the wire path on the diagram.

Start

66 String of Christmas lights

Nothing draws your attention more than a strand of twinkling Christmas lights. These are perfect for bracelets and make beautiful borders on cards and scrapbook pages.

Easy

Bead store
- 30+ dark green beads
- 30 silver beads
- 31 red beads
- 31 green beads
- 31 blue beads
- 31 yellow beads
- 31 pink beads

You will need
- Basic tool kit
- 30 gauge (0.25mm) silver wire

Beading how to
To make the string of Christmas lights, use the basic assembly techniques on pages 18–21 and follow the wire path on the diagram.

1 First, assemble the number of lights you need for your project, as usual.

2 Then string them all along a separate piece of silver wire, adding 5 dark green beads in between each light, as in the pattern.

3 You can make your strand of lights as long or short as you like!

Key for the patterns: Blue is the left-hand end of the wire ● Red is the right-hand end of the wire

67 Christmas ornaments

What tree is complete without heaps of colorful ornaments? You can use larger beads with this pattern and make your own beaded ornaments, or make them as gifts for everyone you know.

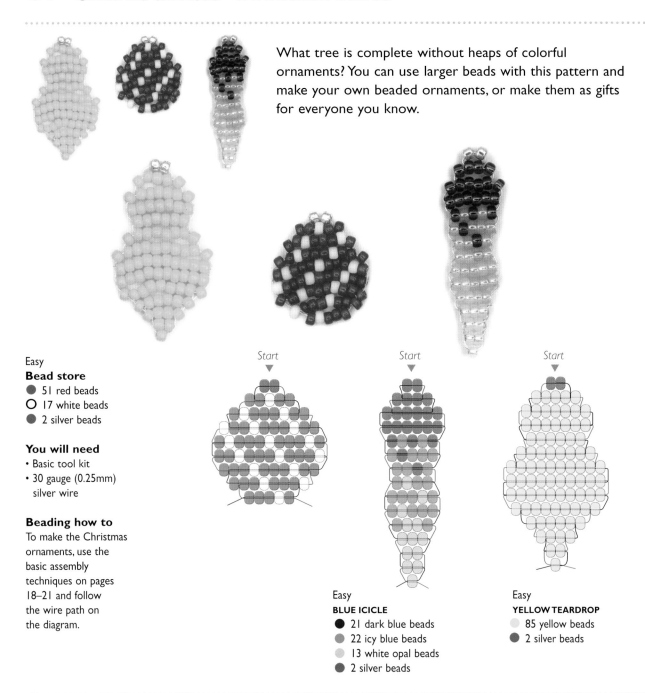

Easy
Bead store
- ● 51 red beads
- ○ 17 white beads
- ● 2 silver beads

You will need
- Basic tool kit
- 30 gauge (0.25mm) silver wire

Beading how to
To make the Christmas ornaments, use the basic assembly techniques on pages 18–21 and follow the wire path on the diagram.

Start

Start

Start

Easy
BLUE ICICLE
- ● 21 dark blue beads
- ● 22 icy blue beads
- ● 13 white opal beads
- ● 2 silver beads

Easy
YELLOW TEARDROP
- ● 85 yellow beads
- ● 2 silver beads

68 Stockings

Let's not forget to hang our stockings before bed on Christmas Eve! I wonder what treasures we will find inside on Christmas morning.

Easy

Bead store

RED/GREEN

○ 10 white beads
● 26 red beads
● 8 green beads

You will need
• Basic tool kit
• 30 gauge (0.25mm) silver wire

Beading how to
To make the stockings, use the basic assembly techniques on pages 18–21 and follow the wire path on the diagram.

Start ▼

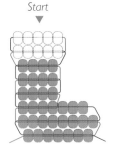

RED AND WHITE

○ 10 white beads
● 34 red beads

RED AND GREEN STRIPED

○ 10 white beads
● 17 red beads
● 17 green beads

69 Reindeer

This little reindeer has a red nose; perhaps it is Rudolph, here to pay us a visit from the North Pole. He would look so cute in Christmas cards and on scrapbook pages!

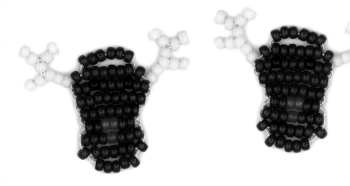

Easy

Bead store

● 58 brown beads
○ 20 beige beads
● 3 red beads
● 2 black beads

You will need
• Basic tool kit
• 30 gauge (0.25mm) silver wire

Beading how to
To make the reindeer, use the basic assembly techniques on pages 18–21 and follow the wire path on the diagram.

Start ▼

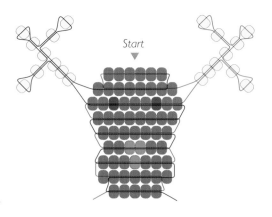

Key for the patterns: Blue is the left-hand end of the wire ● Red is the right-hand end of the wire

70 Santa

Ho ho ho! Why it's Santa Claus himself! I hope everyone has been good all year so that he can leave lots of surprises!

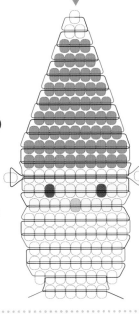

Easy

Bead store
- 🔴 62 red beads
- ⚪ 67 white beads
- 16 peach beads
- ⚫ 2 black beads
- 🔵 1 pink bead

You will need
- Basic tool kit
- 30 gauge (0.25mm) silver wire

Beading how to
To make Santa, use the basic assembly techniques on pages 18–21 and follow the wire path on the diagram.

71 Gingerbread man

It is so much fun to bake and decorate your own gingerbread cookies for Santa! These little beaded versions are perfect for unique holiday-themed jewelry.

Easy

Bead store
- 🔴 106 brown beads
- ⚪ 12 white beads
- ⚫ 2 black beads
- 🔴 1 red bead
- 1 yellow bead
- 🟢 1 green bead

You will need
- Basic tool kit
- 30 gauge (0.25mm) silver wire

Beading how to

1 Make the gingerbread man's body using the techniques on pages 18–21 and follow the wire path on the diagram.

2 After the body is finished, use a separate piece of wire to construct one arm.

3 String the extra wire from the arm through the body as shown in the pattern.

4 Finish the second arm on the opposite side of the body.

5 Secure the wire end as usual.

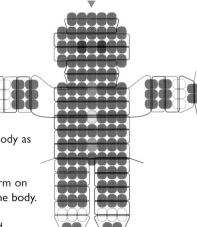

Once upon a time

If you're looking for fairytale trinkets, this is the chapter for you. Just have a look over all these wonderful designs you can try out:

72 Carriage

There is no better mode of transportation for royalty. This beautiful sparkling carriage is heading for the royal ball at the castle—better hop on!

Easy

Bead store
- 58 pink beads
- ○ 16 crystal beads
- ● 25 silver beads
- ○ 1 crystal bicone bead (crystal AB)
- 2 pink glass rounds (crystal AB)

You will need
- Basic tool kit
- 30 gauge (0.25mm) silver wire

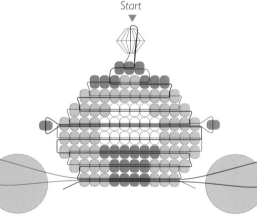

Start

Beading how to

To make the carriage, use the basic assembly techniques on pages 18–21 and follow the wire path on the diagram as usual, substituting a crystal bicone and glass rounds as needed.

Key for the patterns: Blue is the left-hand end of the wire

73 Castle

74 Magic wand

What a stunning shimmering castle! It looks like all the lights are on inside in anticipation of the royal ball. Can you see the prince and princess dancing inside?

These little beaded wands work up very quickly. They are perfect for earrings or to use in fairytale-themed projects. The color possibilities are endless.

Intermediate

Bead store

- ● 81 x 6/0 pink beads
- ● 57 x 6/0 purple beads
- ● 25 x 6/0 yellow beads

You will need
- Basic tool kit
- 30 gauge (0.25mm) silver wire

Beading how to

1 To make the castle, construct the middle section first using the techniques on pages 18–21 and follow the wire path on the diagram.

2 While you are constructing the two outer sections, in the process of beading, attach them to the middle section as shown in the pattern.

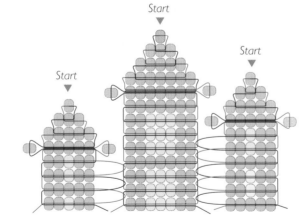

Start

Start

Start

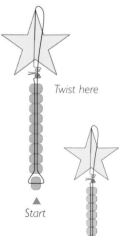

Easy

Bead store

- ● 10 pink, purple, or green beads
- ● 1 small yellow glass star bead

You will need
- Basic tool kit
- 30 gauge (0.25mm) silver wire

Beading how to

To make magic wand, use the basic assembly techniques on pages 18–21 and follow the wire path on the diagram.

Twist here

Start

75 Fairy

76 Glass slipper

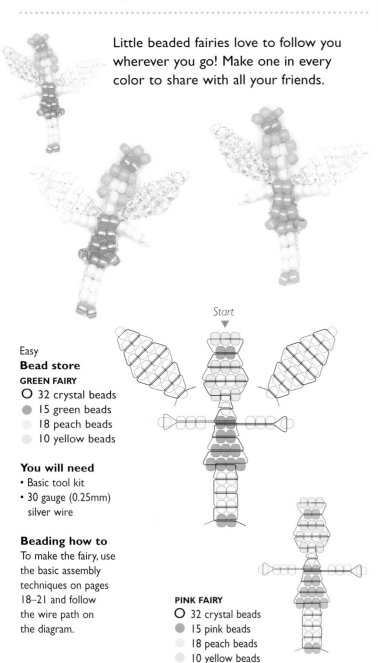

Little beaded fairies love to follow you wherever you go! Make one in every color to share with all your friends.

Oh no! Cinderella has left her slipper behind! Better hurry and bead up some more before the clock strikes midnight!

Easy
Bead store
GREEN FAIRY

○ 32 crystal beads
● 15 green beads
● 18 peach beads
● 10 yellow beads

You will need
• Basic tool kit
• 30 gauge (0.25mm) silver wire

Beading how to
To make the fairy, use the basic assembly techniques on pages 18–21 and follow the wire path on the diagram.

PINK FAIRY

○ 32 crystal beads
● 15 pink beads
● 18 peach beads
● 10 yellow beads

Intermediate
Bead store
● 75 icy blue beads
● 1 x 5mm blue heart

You will need
• Basic tool kit
• 30 gauge (0.25mm) silver wire

Beading how to
To make the slipper, use the basic assembly techniques on pages 18–21 and follow the wire path on the diagram.

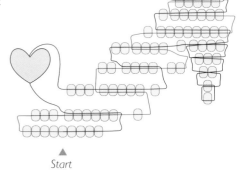

Start

Key for the patterns: Blue is the left-hand end of the wire ● Red is the right-hand end of the wire

77 Princess

This princess looks absolutely exquisite and she is ready to host a splendid ball. Her dress can be made using any number of pretty colored beads.

Easy
Bead store
- ◯ 107 blue beads
- ◯ 45 white beads
- ◯ 25 peach beads
- ◯ 31 yellow beads
- ● 6 black beads

You will need
- Basic tool kit
- 30 gauge (0.25mm) silver wire

Beading how to
To make the princess, use the basic assembly techniques on pages 18–21 and follow the wire path on the diagram.

78 Prince

The handsome prince is ready to escort the beautiful princess to the ball. This little beaded figure is perfect paired up with the princess and used on cards and fairytale scrapbook pages.

Easy
Bead store
- ● 37 red beads
- ◯ 45 beige beads
- ◯ 20 peach beads
- ◯ 13 yellow/gold beads
- ● 19 black beads
- ◯ 2 white beads

You will need
- Basic tool kit
- 30 gauge (0.25mm) silver wire

Beading how to
To make the prince, use the basic assembly techniques on pages 18–21 and follow the wire path on the diagram.

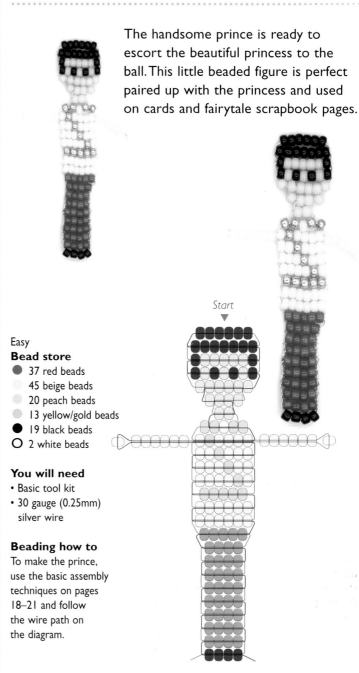

79 Tiny flowers

Bead up a whole bunch of these tiny little flowers using all different colors. They will be the perfect addition to your beaded kingdom!

Easy

Bead store
- ● 6 purple, pink, blue,
- ○ or white beads
- ● 6 green beads
- ○ 1 yellow bead

You will need
- Basic tool kit
- 30 gauge (0.25mm) silver wire

Beading how to
To make the tiny flowers, use the basic assembly techniques on pages 18–21 and follow the wire path on the diagram.

Start ▲

80 Crown

No princess can be without a crown. This is an adorable project which can be turned into a ring, the perfect gift for any princess! You can change the colored jewels to match birthstones.

Easy

Bead store
SILVER
- ● 38+ silver beads
- ● 3 purple beads
- ● 2 pink beads

You will need
- Basic tool kit
- 30 gauge (0.25mm) silver wire

Beading how to
To make the crown, use the basic assembly techniques on pages 18–21 and follow the wire path on the diagram.

Start ▼

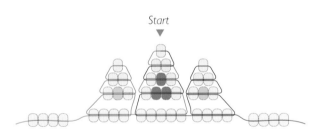

Add the number of beads you would like to complete the band of the crown.

GOLD
- ○ 38+ gold beads
- ● 3 purple beads
- ● 2 pink beads

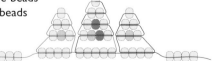

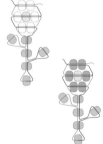

Key for the patterns: Blue is the left-hand end of the wire ● Red is the right-hand end of the wire

Be my Valentine

Choose from the multitude of charms in this chapter to show off your romantic side:

81 Diamond ring

This beautiful beaded ring is the perfect embellishment to include on Valentine's Day and wedding cards. Of course, you can change the stone as well.

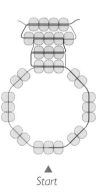

Easy

Bead store

- 12 crystal/pale ice transparent beads
- 20 gold beads

You will need

- Basic tool kit
- 30 gauge (0.25mm) silver wire

Beading how to

To make the diamond ring, use the basic assembly techniques on pages 18–21, and follow the wire path on the diagram.

▲
Start

82 Love letter

Leave these little beaded trinkets lying around for a special someone to find! A love letter from a secret admirer is a wonderful surprise!

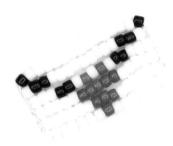

Easy

Bead store

○ 69 white beads

● 10 black beads

● 11 red beads

You will need

• Basic tool kit

• 30 gauge (0.25mm) silver wire

Beading how to

To make the love letter, use the basic assembly techniques on pages 18–21 and follow the wire path on the diagram.

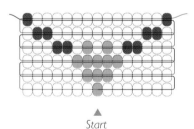

▲
Start

83 Hearts

These tiny hearts are a quick project with infinite potential: Earrings for Valentine's Day, charm bracelets for a friend, or embellishments for an endless variety of cards and scrapbook pages.

Easy

Bead store

● 30 red, pink, or lavender beads

You will need

• Basic tool kit

• 30 gauge (0.25mm) silver wire

Beading how to

To make the hearts, use the basic assembly techniques on pages 18–21 and follow the wire path on the diagram.

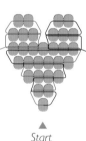

▲
Start

84 Flower

Make up a dozen of these lovely red flowers to give to someone special. A bouquet of rainbow-colored flowers would be just as striking!

Easy

Bead store
- 28 red beads
- 19 green beads

You will need
- Basic tool kit
- 30 gauge (0.25mm) silver wire

Beading how to
To make the flower, use the basic assembly techniques on pages 18–21 and follow the wire path on the diagram.

▲
Start

85 Love bugs

These adorable little bugs make a fun Valentine's surprise for children. Hide them in secret places and see who can find them!

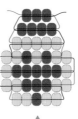

Easy

Bead store

PINK/BLACK BUG
- 20 pink beads
- 18 black beads

You will need
- Basic tool kit
- 30 gauge (0.25mm) silver wire

Beading how to
To make the love bugs, use the basic assembly techniques on pages 18–21 and follow the wire path on the diagram.

▲
Start

RED/BLACK BUG
- 20 red beads
- 18 black beads

PINK/LAVENDER BUG
- 20 pink beads
- 16 lavender beads
- 2 black beads

PURPLE/PINK BUG
- 16 pink beads
- 20 purple beads
- 2 black beads

86 Box of chocolates with a hinged lid

A delicious box of chocolates is the perfect gift for Valentine's Day. With this beaded box, you can keep them around forever!

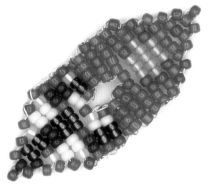

Easy
Bead store
- 94 red beads
- 11 dark brown beads
- 16 pearlescent brown beads
- 12 cream beads
- 6 light pink beads
- 11 dark pink beads
- 2 green beads

You will need
- Basic tool kit
- 30 gauge (0.25mm) silver wire

Beading how to
1 To make the box of chocolates first assemble each piece of the box, the base and the lid, by using the techniques on pages 18–21 and following the wire path on the diagram.

2 Next, use two new pieces of wire to attach the lid to the base as shown, with the green lines in the pattern.

3 This creates a hinged box that can open and shut!

Base

Start

Lid

Start

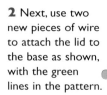

87 Raspberry cream

This yummy little treat beads up quickly and would look great on any project for Valentine's Day or for a chocolate-lover.

Easy
Bead store
- 6 dark pink beads
- 22 opaque brown beads

You will need
- Basic tool kit
- 30 gauge (0.25mm) silver wire

Start

Beading how to
To make the raspberry cream, use the basic assembly techniques on pages 18–21 and follow the wire path on the diagram.

88 Glass of wine & glass of champagne

What better way to celebrate a special occasion than with a glass of red wine or bubbly champagne?

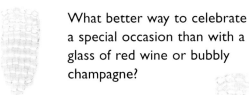

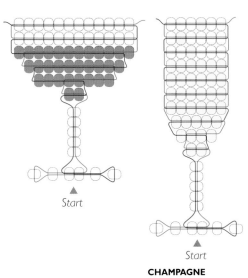

Easy

Bead store

WINE

● 32 deep red beads

O 35 crystal beads

You will need
- Basic tool kit
- 30 gauge (0.25mm) silver wire

Beading how to

To make the glass of wine and the glass of champagne, use the basic assembly techniques on pages 18–21 and follow the wire path on the diagram.

▲ *Start*

CHAMPAGNE

38 light amber beads

O 26 crystal beads

89 Wine bottle

Change the color of the beads used in this wine bottle to change its contents. You can fill up your mini wine cellar with these colorful treats!

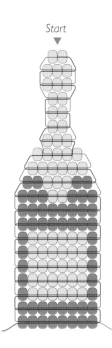

Easy

Bead store

● 52 green beads

63 gold or yellow beads

You will need
- Basic tool kit
- 30 gauge (0.25mm) silver wire

Beading how to

To make the wine bottle, use the basic assembly techniques on pages 18–21 and follow the wire path on the diagram.

Start ▼

Wonderland tea party

In this chapter you can get yourself into the party mood and start celebrating with these cute trinkets:

90 Alice

Alice will be our host at this silly and exciting birthday tea party in Wonderland!

Easy

Bead store
- 37 blue beads
- ○ 39 white beads
- 23 peach beads
- 19 yellow beads
- ● 6 black beads

You will need
- Basic tool kit
- 30 gauge (0.25mm) silver wire

Beading how to
To make Alice, use the basic assembly techniques on pages 18–21 and follow the wire path on the diagram.

Start

Key for the patterns: ● Blue is the left-hand end of the wire

91 Balloons

One thing you need a lot of at birthday parties is balloons. You can make these up in any colors you like to match your own birthday color scheme.

Easy
Bead store
- 33 purple, pink, or blue beads

You will need
- Basic tool kit
- 30 gauge (0.25mm) silver wire

Beading how to
To make the balloons, use the basic assembly techniques on pages 18–21 and follow the wire path on the diagram.

Start
▼

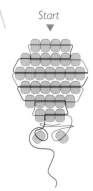

92 Mad Hatter's cake

This is one crazy cake! Bursting with bright colors and stars, this is sure to get some attention!

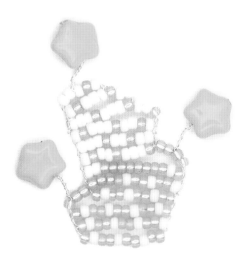

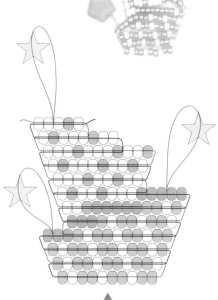

▲
Start

Intermediate
Bead store
- 37 pink beads
- 16 blue beads
- 14 purple beads
- ○ 58 white beads
- 3 small yellow glass star beads

You will need
- Basic tool kit
- 30 gauge (0.25mm) silver wire

Beading how to
1 To make the Mad Hatter's birthday cake, assemble the base of the cake as usual by using the techniques on pages 18–21 and follow the wire path on the diagram.

2 Next, add the stars in varying places on the cake as indicated in the pattern chart.

3 To make it so that these stars appear to be bursting out of the cake, string the star on a separate wire, twist the wire to the desired length, then weave the wire ends into the base of the cake.

4 You may need to arrange the wire to bend in the direction that you desire.

5 Repeat this with each of the three stars.

93 Party hats

Everyone will have fun wearing party hats! Make up several in lots of different colors and designs so that everyone can have their favorite colors!

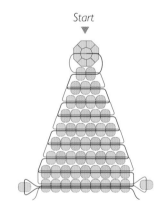

Easy

Bead store
- 31 pink beads
- 24 purple beads
- 1 x 4mm pink crystal bead

You will need
- Basic tool kit
- 30 gauge (0.25mm) silver wire

Beading how to
To make the party hats, use the basic assembly techniques on pages 18–21 and follow the wire path on the diagram.

Start

94 Presents

What could be inside these beautiful packages? They would make great favors to give out at birthday parties.

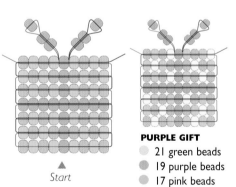

Easy

Bead store
- 21 blue beads
- 24 pink beads
- 24 purple beads

You will need
- Basic tool kit
- 30 gauge (0.25mm) silver wire

Beading how to
To make the presents, use the basic assembly techniques on pages 18–21 and follow the wire path on the diagram.

▲
Start

PURPLE GIFT
- 21 green beads
- 19 purple beads
- 17 pink beads
- 12 yellow beads

TIP
Change the colors to red and green and you have an extra item for your Christmas motifs!

95 Teacup

Do you take sugar in your tea? These cute little teacups would make adorable ornaments for all the tea lovers out there!

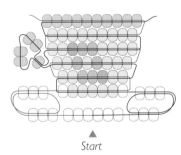

▲
Start

Intermediate
Bead store
- 30 yellow beads
- ○ 20 white beads
- 15 pink beads
- 6 purple beads
- 2 green beads

You will need
- Basic tool kit
- 30 gauge (0.25mm) silver wire

Beading how to
To make the teacup, use the basic assembly techniques on pages 18–21 and follow the wire path on the diagram.

96 Teapot

What flavor of tea do you prefer? Peppermint? Rose? I'm sure every flavor imaginable is being served up at this tea party!

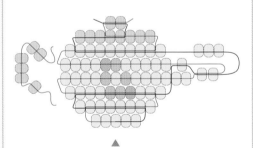

▲
Start

Intermediate
Bead store
- 56 yellow beads
- 16 pink beads
- 5 purple beads
- 2 green beads

You will need
- Basic tool kit
- 30 gauge (0.25mm) silver wire

Beading how to
To make the teapot, use the basic assembly techniques on pages 18–21 and follow the wire path on the diagram.

97 Candle

It's time to blow out the candles. How many will you need on your next birthday cake?

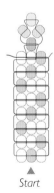

▲
Start

Easy
Bead store
- 8 pink, blue, or purple beads
- ○ 16 white beads
- 3 orange beads
- 1 yellow beads

You will need
- Basic tool kit
- 30 gauge (0.25mm) silver wire

Beading how to
To make the candles, use the basic assembly techniques on pages 18–21 and follow the wire path on the diagram.

Around the world

This chapter is sure to inspire you to travel the world. Choose from these fantastic charms and begin your journey:

98 Globe

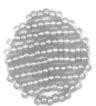

Where will your travels take you? On a safari? To the rainforest? With these little beaded motifs, the world is at your fingertips!

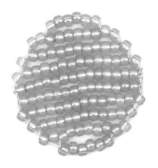

Easy

Bead store
- 63 blue beads
- 49 green beads

You will need
- Basic tool kit
- 30 gauge (0.25mm) silver wire

Beading how to
To make the globe, use the basic assembly techniques on pages 18–21 and follow the wire path on the diagram.

Start ▼

99 Suitcase

It's time to pack our bags. This cute little beaded motif would be great used on travel and vacation scrapbook pages.

Easy

Bead store
- 71 light brown beads
- 22 brown beads
- 11 yellow beads
- 6 blue beads
- 6 red beads
- 5 orange beads

You will need
- Basic tool kit
- 30 gauge (0.25mm) silver wire

Beading how to
To make the suitcase, use the basic assembly techniques on pages 18–21 and follow the wire path on the diagram.

▲ *Start*

Key for the patterns: Blue is the left-hand end of the wire ● Red is the right-hand end of the wire

100 Hot air balloon

Float around the world in this colorful balloon. Who knows what exciting places it will take us to!

Easy

Bead store

- 18 red beads
- 17 orange beads
- 16 yellow beads
- 15 light green beads
- 10 green beads
- 12 blue beads
- 9 purple beads
- 8 brown beads

You will need
- Basic tool kit
- 30 gauge (0.25mm) silver wire

Beading how to

1 To make the hot air balloon, assemble the balloon by using the techniques on pages 18–21 and following the wire path on the diagram.

2 When you get to the last row of the balloon, with four beads, let some extra wire out before proceeding with the first row of brown beads in the basket.

3 Assemble the basket as usual and secure the wire ends.

Start ▼

101 Maracas

These maracas are a fun instrument that will add plenty of color to your vacation scrapbook pages! A fun pair of earrings could be made from these as well.

Easy

Bead store

PINK MARACA
- 15 beige beads
- 11 yellow beads
- 9 blue beads
- 19 pink beads
- 14 green beads

You will need
- Basic tool kit
- 30 gauge (0.25mm) silver wire

Beading how to

To make the maracas, use the basic assembly techniques on pages 18–21 and follow the wire path on the diagram.

Start ▼

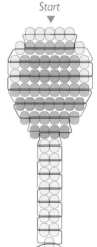

RED MARACA
- 15 beige beads
- 26 red beads
- 11 yellow beads
- 8 orange beads
- 8 blue beads

102 Matryoshka doll

These little Matryoshka, or nesting, dolls have been around for centuries in Russia. It will be fun to bead up several in all your favorite color combinations.

Easy

Bead store
- 🔴 52 red beads
- ⚪ 45 yellow beads
- ⚫ 29 blue beads
- ⚪ 11 peach beads
- 🟤 12 brown beads
- 🟢 13 green beads

You will need
- Basic tool kit
- 30 gauge (0.25mm) silver wire

Beading how to
To make the Matryoshka doll, use the basic assembly techniques on pages 18–21 and follow the wire path on the diagram.

Start ▼

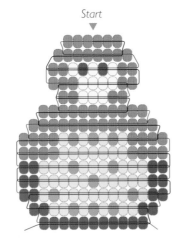

103 Paper lanterns

These Chinese paper lanterns are popular at parties. They bring a beautiful soft glow to the area. These beaded lanterns will lend a beautiful air of style to any Asian-themed project.

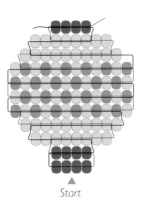
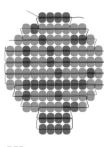

Easy

Bead store

YELLOW
- ⚪ 60 yellow beads
- 🔴 24 red beads
- ⚫ 12 black beads

You will need
- Basic tool kit
- 30 gauge (0.25mm) silver wire

Beading how to
To make the paper lanterns, use the basic assembly techniques on pages 18–21 and follow the wire path on the diagram.

Start ▲

RED
- 🔴 60 red beads
- ⚫ 36 black beads

GREEN
- 🟢 64 green beads
- ⚪ 20 yellow beads
- ⚫ 12 black beads

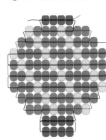

Key for the patterns: Blue is the left-hand end of the wire ● Red is the right-hand end of the wire

104 Eiffel Tower

Bonjour! What is a trip to Paris without visiting the Eiffel Tower? It is one of the most recognizable structures in the world.

Intermediate

Bead store
● 87 gray beads

You will need
• Basic tool kit
• 30 gauge (0.25mm) silver wire

Beading how to

1 First complete Section 1 of the pattern by using the techniques on pages 18–21 and follow the wire path on the diagram.

2 Next, complete Section 2.

3 After Section 2 is finished, do not cut the extra wire.

4 Use the extra wire from this section to attach Section 1 and Section 2.

Start

Section 1

Section 2

Start

105 Queen's guard

The changing of the guard is a spectacular event not to be missed! This little beaded guard is perfect if you can't make the trip to the palace.

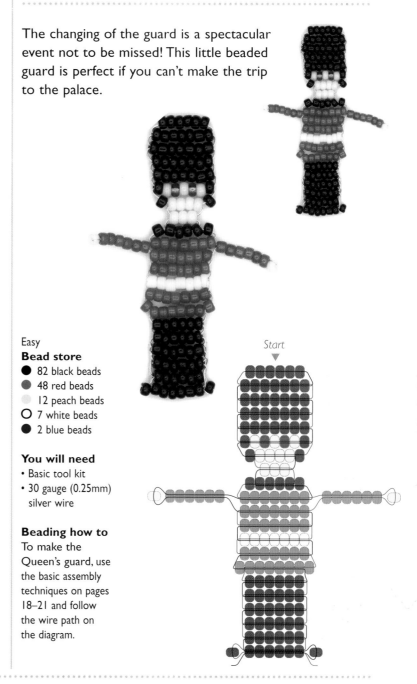

Easy

Bead store
● 82 black beads
● 48 red beads
○ 12 peach beads
○ 7 white beads
● 2 blue beads

You will need
• Basic tool kit
• 30 gauge (0.25mm) silver wire

Beading how to
To make the Queen's guard, use the basic assembly techniques on pages 18–21 and follow the wire path on the diagram.

Start

Section 4:
Projects

Garden party

Beaded miniatures have many uses, from eye-catching earrings to useful everyday items such as drink markers.

Pretty pin
Choose a few complementary fabric swatches and simply hand-stitch some of your favorite charms onto the layered swatches. You can either sew or glue these onto a bar pin (see page 15).

Floral headband

To create this floral fascinator, just wrap wire around a length of beads to attach it to the headband. Next, take your chosen flower charms and add some beaded loops to them. To bring it all together, just weave some more wire between the charms and the headband.

Tutti-frutti earrings

The key to these earrings is simple jump rings. Attach one to each trinket (see page 21) and then close the jump ring around one of the loops in the earring chain.

Drink marker

These are so easy to make and will ensure you never lose your drink again. Simply attach a jump ring (see page 21) to your chosen charm and then link the jump ring to a large split ring.

Charming gifts

Adding beaded trinkets to fabric cards creates a wonderful keepsake. You can also use your miniatures in gift projects and give them on any holiday or occasion.

Valentine kilt pin
This kilt pin has been adorned with beaded miniature hearts. You too can make this for someone you love by simply adding jump rings and head pins (see page 21).

Cake-stand bookmark
To create this delightful bookmark, you can either make your own embroidered background, or buy a ready-made one and simply hand-stitch your charms onto it.

Season's Greetings

Christmas card
If you feel like sending some extra special cards this Christmas, why not add some of your favorite beaded designs? Simply glue or hand-stitch them on.

Birthday card
With all the beaded patterns in this book, you'll be able to tailor any birthday card to anyone you like, whether they're a nature fan or love indulging in tea and cake!

Happy Birthday

Sun, sea, and accessories

There are many items of jewelry that lend themselves perfectly to beaded charms. Pendants are great for displaying your trinkets, while earrings will add a bit of fun to any outfit.

Fairytale appliqué

You can group your chosen charms together as pins and create a mini scene. You can also add fabrics to enhance your designs, such as giving your princess a fuller skirt with some organza.

Ice cream cone earrings

Make yourslf some cool earrings by adding jump rings (see page 21) to each ice cream cone and then simply attach the rings to ear wires.

Flip-flop pendant

Once you have added a jump ring (see page 21) to your chosen charm, all you need to do is fasten it to a necklace. You could use a chain, some cord, or even a ribbon.

Framed collections

Shadow boxes are a simple yet stylish way to display your favorite groupings of miniatures. You can arrange them by theme, color, or simply gather all of your favorites together.

Beautiful bugs

Once you have selected your shadow box (left), just pick out a fabric background and glue or hand-stitch your trinkets to it. Next, secure the fabric to the frame and admire your work!

Animal buttons

If you want to add something more to your shadow box you could mount a group of miniatures on some over-sized buttons.

Sea charm bracelet

In addition to featuring your fish trinket you can add some sparkly beads in ocean colors. By sticking with just one charm you'll really make him the star of the show!

Charm bracelets

These are a great way to carry your favorite beaded trinkets with you all of the time. You can add as few, or as many, as you like! To make each bracelet, all you need are some jump rings (see page 21), a chain bracelet, and head pins (see page 15) for adding special beads.

Sweetheart charm bracelet

You can use charm bracelets to indicate your mood. If you're feeling loved-up, why not make up this cute sweetheart bracelet for all to see?

Personalized charm bracelet

If you want to give a great gift you should make a themed charm bracelet. Bead up your friend's favorite designs and give them a truly unique personalized present.

Mirror, mirror ...

There is no doubt about it, you'll definitely be
the fairest of them all wearing any of these
fantastic beaded accessories.

Flower rings
Why not customize your choice of colors on these
daisy rings? That way you can have a ring to match any
outfit. Once you have your charm just use jeweler's
glue to attach it to a ring blank (see page 15).

Butterfly brooches
You can bead up lots of these simple butterflies in a variety of colors. Once you have attached them to bar pins (see page 15) you can mix and match your color combinations and fasten them onto hats and clothing.

Fairy necklace
This necklace will display any beaded trinket in all its glory. Once you have selected your charm and necklace you just need a jump ring to link them together (see page 21).

Index

Page numbers in **bold** refer to assembly instructions.

Resources
USA
Art Beads
www.artbeads.com

Auntie's Beads
www.auntiesbeads.com

Fire Mountain Gems and Beads
www.firemountaingems.com

Jerry Smith Beads
www.jsbeads.com

Jewelry Supply
www.jewelrysupply.com

Kandra's Beads
www.kandrasbeads.com

Beaded Impressions Inc.
www.abeadstore.com

Shipwreck Beads
www.shipwreck.com

Global Beads
www.globalbeads.com

Just Beads
www.justbeads.com

UK
Spangles
www.spangles4beads.co.uk

P J Minerals
www.beads.co.uk

Creative Beadcraft
www.creativebeadcraft.co.uk

GJ Beads
www.gjbeads.co.uk

Beadworks
www.beadworks.co.uk

International Craft
www.internationalcraft.com

The Brighton Bead Shop
www.beadsunlimited.co.uk

Australia/New Zealand
The Bead Bar
www.thebeadbar.com.au

The Bead Company
www.beadco.com.au

Bead Gallery
www.beads.co.nz

Beads Glorious Beads
www.beadsgloriousbeads.com

Bead Needs
www.beadneeds.com.au

Credits
All photographs and illustrations
are the copyright of Quarto
Publishing plc. While every
effort has been made to credit
contributors, Quarto would like
to apologize should there have
been any omissions or errors –
and would be pleased to make the
appropriate correction for future
editions of the book.